A YEAR WITH
AMERICA'S FOUNDERS

A YEAR WITH
AMERICA'S FOUNDERS

*365 Days of Wisdom and Insight from Our
Founding Fathers*

Compiled by Jay A. Parry

STONEWELL PRESS

Cover design by Nathaniel J. Parry

ISBN 978-1-62730-116-9

Published by Stonewell Press
Salt Lake City, Utah
stonewellpress.com

Other Books Published by Stonewell Press

Back to First Principles: A Conversation with George Washington, *by Jay A. Parry*

Classic Essays on Political Economy, *by M. Frederic Bastiat*

Common Sense, *by Thomas Paine*

Democracy in America, Abridged, 2 Volumes in 1, *by Alexis de Tocqueville*

On Liberty, *by John Stuart Mill*

Philip Dru, Administrator, *by Edward Mandell House*

That Which Is Seen and That Which Is Not Seen: The Unintended Consequences of Government Spending, *by M. Frederic Bastiat*

The Federalist Papers, *by Alexander Hamilton, James Madison, and John Jay*

The Law, *by M. Frederic Bastiat*

The Life of George Washington, *by David Ramsay*

The Second Treatise of Civil Government, *by John Locke*

The Very Best of the Federalist Papers, *by Alexander Hamilton, James Madison, and John Jay*

The Way to Wealth, *by Benjamin Franklin*

The Wealth of Nations, Abridged, *by Adam Smith*

CONTENTS

INTRODUCTION

In 1787, what may have been the most impressive group of statesmen ever to assemble gathered in the hot, muggy Philadelphia summer to create the foundational document for a new government. The principles underlying that document, the Constitution of the United States of America, established a nation that became the most free, most prosperous, most powerful nation in the history of the world.

Now, in some vital respects, America seems to have lost her way.

A struggling economy, national debt, constant overreach by the federal government, utter disregard for the Constitution by (seemingly) all three branches of the national government, disdain from other nations, widespread immorality—all these challenges and many more tell us that we have strayed from the founding principles of our nation.

If only we could be renewed in our understandings of the philosophy and vision of our Founders.

This book will help to strengthen that understanding. If you will read and ponder just one quotation a day, the founding principles of our nation will begin to distill more fully upon your mind and heart. You will begin to internalize what our Founding Fathers thought and said. And the more people who are renewed in those principles, the stronger our nation will become.

Of course, your reading can start anywhere in the book, and you certainly don't have to read in order. You don't even have to limit yourself to a quotation a day!

Unfortunately, some famous quotations attributed to the Founders actually weren't said by them at all. Because the internet (and certain books) perpetuate the use of spurious quotations, the editor took care to verify all quotations in this book, and a source is attached to each.

The quotations in this collection have been presented verbatim, as they are found in the original documents, with the following exceptions: archaic spellings have been standardized, British spellings have been Americanized, occasional punctuation has been added or deleted for clarity, capitalization has been modernized, and "&" has been changed to "and."

America's Founding Fathers comprise a rather large group that could consist of all the signers of the Declaration of Independence (56 men), all the signers of the Constitution (39 men, of whom 6 also signed the Declaration), and various other leaders, writers, and activists. Because of limitations on space, however, this book includes only eight of the most prominent of those men. Here is a brief introduction to each, arranged in chronological order by the date of their birth:

Benjamin Franklin (1706–1790) was an inventor, statesman, diplomat, publisher, and best-selling author. He was instrumental in founding the University of Pennsylvania, was governor of Pennsylvania, and served for many years as America's minister to France. There, he was able to negotiate significant financial support for the American Revolutionary War. Franklin was on the committee that wrote the Declaration of Independence and was a key delegate to the Constitutional Convention of 1787. He was famous for his wit, and a number of his sayings remain current in our culture. He was one of

the best-known and most respected of Americans, both
at home and abroad.

Samuel Adams (1722–1803) was a political leader
and firebrand from Massachusetts. He spoke out vehe-
mently against the British taxation of Americans without
representation and was influential in coordinating a resistance movement among the thirteen colonies. His efforts
helped lead to the Boston Tea Party of 1773. Adams was
a member of the Continental Congress for eight years,
where he argued for separation from Great Britain, and
he was a signer of the Declaration of Independence. He
later became governor of Massachusetts. Most of his
important writings were published in newspapers under
pseudonyms, a common practice of the time.

George Washington (1732–1799) was a well-known
military figure even before the Revolutionary War. He
attended the First and Second Continental Congresses,
where he strongly supported American independence,
and in 1775 was named as the commanding general of
the American armies. He was chosen president of the
Constitutional Convention of 1787, and, in 1789, was
unanimously elected the first president of the United
States. He was praised by his contemporaries for twice
stepping down from the pinnacle of power, first, for resigning his commission as commander-in-chief after the
Revolutionary War; and second, for leaving the presi-
dency after serving two terms. He was widely regarded
as a powerful leader and a man of unassailable integrity.

John Adams (1735–1826) was an articulate advocate
of America's independence. He was a repeat delegate
to the Continental Congress and was a key member of
the committee assigned to write the Declaration of Independence. In the 1780s, he served as U.S. minister
to the Netherlands and to England, where he helped
negotiate America's peace treaty with Great Britain. He
was a prolific writer, publishing such influential books on

political theory as *Thoughts on Government* and *Defence of the Constitutions of Government of the United States of America*. Adams served as first vice president and second president of the United States. In his old age (he lived to age 90), he continued to write voluminously, tirelessly expounding the principles held by the founders of America.

Thomas Paine (1737–1809) was a political thinker and writer with tremendous influence on citizens and leaders in the United States. He was author of the influential political pamphlet *Common Sense*, which was the best-selling book of its time and which helped persuade Americans that they should establish independence from Great Britain. Of Paine's work, John Adams said, "Without the pen of the author of *Common Sense*, the sword of Washington would have been raised in vain." Later, his *American Crisis* inspired Americans to continue their cause through the war. He also served in the rebel army and donated the profits from *Common Sense* to help supply that army. Paine's book *The Rights of Man*, published in two parts in 1791 and 1792, sold nearly a million copies.

Thomas Jefferson (1743–1826) was a delegate to the Second Continental Congress, where he was asked to be the principal author of the Declaration of Independence. During the Revolutionary War, he served as second governor of Virginia. In the latter part of the 1780s, he was U.S. minister to France. He was America's first secretary of state, second vice president, and third president, serving two terms. As president, he was responsible for doubling the geographic size of the nation through the Louisiana Purchase. Later, he founded the University of Virginia. Jefferson was a powerful writer, and his *Notes on Virginia* was influential in France and England, as well as the United States. Both Jefferson and Adams died on the fiftieth anniversary of the signing of the Declaration of

Independence, July 4, 1826.

James Madison (1751–1836) is known as the "Father of the Constitution." He was a key figure in the Constitutional Convention of 1787, kept a record of the debates, and authored and championed the Bill of Rights. Madison was one of the primary authors of the influential *Federalist Papers*, which helped to explain and promote the new Constitution to the general public—and to leaders of the states—prior to the Constitution's ratification. He was an early and crucial member of Congress, secretary of state under Thomas Jefferson, and third president of the United States. Though he was sickly through much of his life, Madison was the last of the Founding Fathers to die, in 1836 at age 85.

Alexander Hamilton (1755–1804) was the chief staff aide to General George Washington during the Revolutionary War. After the war he served in the Confederation Congress, founded the Bank of New York, and helped influence Congress to call for the Constitutional Convention of 1787. He was named as a delegate to that convention and became a signer of the Constitution. Thereafter, with James Madison and John Jay, he wrote the *Federalist Papers*. Hamilton was America's first secretary of the treasury and established the basis of the nation's financial system. He was killed in a duel with Aaron Burr, who at that time was vice president of the United States.

Of course, there were prominent dissenting points of view during America's founding era. But, as has been said, history is generally written by the victors, and those who espoused the prevailing view of America's founding principles are the men who are represented in this collection.

The statements included in this collection are as wise and timeless as when they were first uttered. All Americans can benefit by deepening their understanding of the principles, beliefs, and political philosophy of their Founders.

JANUARY

January 1

The establishment of civil and religious liberty was the motive which induced me to the field—the object is attained—and it now remains to be my earnest wish and prayer, that the citizens of the United States could make a wise and virtuous use of the blessings placed before them.

> —George Washington to the Reformed German Congregation of New York City, Nov. 27, 1783

January 2

The path we have to pursue [as president] is so quiet that we have nothing scarcely to propose to our legislature. A noiseless course, not meddling with the affairs of others, unattractive of notice, is a mark that society is going on in happiness. If we can prevent the government from wasting the labors of the people, under the pretense of taking care of them, they must become happy.

—Thomas Jefferson to Thomas Cooper, Nov. 29, 1802

January 3

What is wit, or wealth, or form, or learning, when compared with virtue? . . . If we were as industrious to become good as to make ourselves great, we should become really great by being good, and the number of valuable men would be much increased; but it is a grand mistake to think of being great without goodness; and I pronounce it as certain that there was never yet a truly great man that was not at the same time truly virtuous.

—Benjamin Franklin, "The Busy-body," Feb. 18, 1728

January 4

If it be asked, What is the most sacred duty and the greatest source of our security in a republic? The answer would be, An inviolable respect for the Constitution and laws—the first growing out of the last. . . . A sacred respect for the constitutional law is the vital principle, the sustaining energy of a free government.

—Alexander Hamilton, Essay in the *American Daily Advertiser*, Aug. 28, 1794

January 5

The peaceable part of mankind will be continually overrun by the vile and abandoned, while they neglect the means of self-defense. The supposed quietude of a good man allures the ruffian; while on the other hand, arms like laws discourage and keep the invader and the plunderer in awe, and preserve order in the world as well as property. The balance of power is the scale of peace. The same balance would be preserved were all the world destitute of arms, for all would be alike; but since some *will not,* others *dare not* lay them aside. And while a single nation refuses to lay them down, it is proper that all should keep them up. Horrid mischief would ensue were one half the world deprived of the use of them; for while avarice and ambition have a place in the heart of man, the weak will become a prey to the strong. The history of every age and nation establishes these truths, and facts need but little arguments when they prove themselves.

—Thomas Paine, "Thoughts on Defensive War," 1775

January 6

[Congress] are not *to do anything they please* to provide for the general welfare, but only to *lay taxes* for that purpose. To consider the latter phrase not as describing the purpose of the first, but as giving a distinct and independent power to do any act they please which may be good for the Union, would render all the preceding and subsequent enumerations of power completely useless.

It would reduce the whole instrument to a single phrase, that of instituting a Congress with power to do whatever would be for the good of the United States; and as the sole judges of the good or evil, it would be also a power to do whatever evil they please. . . .

Certainly no such universal power was meant to be given them. It [the Constitution] was intended to lace them up straitly within the enumerated powers, and those without which, as means, these powers could not be carried into effect. It is known that the very power now proposed as a means was rejected as an end by the convention which formed the Constitution.

—Thomas Jefferson, "Opinion on National Bank,"
Feb. 15, 1791

January 7

In politics as in philosophy, my tenets are few and simple. The leading one of which, and indeed that which embraces most others, is to be honest and just ourselves and to exact it from others, meddling as little as possible in their affairs where our own are not involved. If this maxim was generally adopted, wars would cease and our swords would soon be converted into reap hooks and our harvests be more peaceful, abundant, and happy.

—George Washington to Dr. James Anderson,
Dec. 24, 1795

January 8

A zeal for different opinions concerning religion, concerning government, and many other points, as well of speculation as of practice; an attachment to different leaders ambitiously contending for pre-eminence and power; or to persons of other descriptions whose fortunes have been interesting to the human passions, have, in turn, divided mankind into parties, inflamed them with mutual animosity, and rendered them much more disposed to vex and oppress each other than to co-operate for their common good.

—James Madison, Federalist No. 10, 1787

January 9

If ever the time should come, when vain and aspiring men shall possess the highest seats in government, our country will stand in need of its experienced patriots to prevent its ruin. There may be more danger of this than some, even of our well-disposed citizens, may imagine. If the people should grant their suffrages to men only because they conceive them to have been friends to the country, without regard to the necessary qualifications for the places they are to fill, the administration of government will become a mere farce, and our public affairs will never be put on the footing of solid security.

—Samuel Adams to James Warren, Oct. 24, 1780

January 10

For my own part, when I am employed in serving others, I do not look upon myself as conferring favors, but as paying debts. In my travels, and since my settlement, I have received much kindness from men, to whom I shall never have any opportunity of making the least direct return. And numberless mercies from God, who is infinitely above being benefited by our services. Those kindnesses from men, I can therefore only return on their fellow men; and I can only shew my gratitude for these mercies from God, by a readiness to help his other children and my brethren. For I do not think that thanks and compliments, though repeated weekly, can discharge our real obligations to each other, and much less those to our Creator.

—Benjamin Franklin to Joseph Huey, June 6, 1753

January 11

This balance between the national and state governments ought to be dwelt on with peculiar attention, as it is of the utmost importance. It forms a double security to the people. If one encroaches on their rights they will find a powerful protection in the other. Indeed, they will both be prevented from overpassing their constitutional limits by a certain rivalship, which will ever subsist between them.

—Alexander Hamilton, New York Ratifying
Convention, June 17, 1788

January 12

There is not a more important and fundamental principle in legislation, than that the ways and means ought always to face the public engagements; that our appropriations should ever go hand in hand with our promises. To say that the United States should be answerable for twenty-five millions of dollars without knowing whether the ways and means can be provided, and without knowing whether those who are to succeed us will think with us on the subject, would be rash and unjustifiable. Sir, in my opinion, it would be hazarding the public faith in a manner contrary to every idea of prudence.

—James Madison, speech in Congress, Apr. 22, 1790

January 13

A wise and frugal government, which shall restrain men from injuring one another, which shall leave them otherwise free to regulate their own pursuits of industry and improvement, and shall not take from the mouth of labor the bread it has earned. This is the sum of good government, and this is necessary to close the circle of our felicities.

—Thomas Jefferson, First Inaugural Address,
Mar. 4, 1801

January 14

This is the most magnificent movement of all [Boston Tea Party]! There is a dignity, a majesty, a sublimity, in this last effort of the patriots that I greatly admire. The people should never rise without doing something to be remembered—something notable and striking. This destruction of the tea is so bold, so daring, so firm, intrepid and inflexible, and it must have so important consequences, and so lasting, that I can't but consider it as an epocha in history!

—John Adams, Diary, Dec. 17, 1773

January 15

When wealth and splendor, instead of fascinating the multitude, excite emotions of disgust; when, instead of drawing forth admiration, it is beheld as an insult upon wretchedness; when the ostentatious appearance it makes serves to call the right of it in question, the case of property becomes critical, and it is only in a system of justice that the possessor can contemplate security.

To remove the danger, it is necessary to remove the antipathies, and this can only be done by making property productive of a national blessing, extending to every individual. When the riches of one man above another shall increase the national fund in the same proportion; when it shall be seen that the prosperity of that fund depends on the prosperity of individuals; when the more riches a man acquires, the better it shall be for the general mass; it is then that antipathies will cease, and property be placed on the permanent basis of national interest and protection.

—Thomas Paine, *Agrarian Justice,* 1797

January 16

As the cool and deliberate sense of the community ought in all governments, and actually will in all free governments ultimately prevail over the views of its rulers; so there are particular moments in public affairs, when the people stimulated by some irregular passion, or some illicit advantage, or misled by the artful misrepresentations of interested men, may call for measures which they themselves will afterwards be the most ready to lament and condemn. In these critical moments, how salutary will be the interference of some temperate and respectable body of citizens, in order to check the misguided career, and to suspend the blow mediated by the people against themselves, until reason, justice and truth, can regain their authority over the public mind?

—James Madison, Federalist No. 63, 1788

January 17

It is the duty of the clergy to accommodate their discourses to the times, to preach against such sins as are most prevalent, and recommend such virtues as are most wanted. For example, if exorbitant ambition and venality are predominant, ought they not to warn their hearers against those vices? If public spirit is much wanted, should they not inculcate this great virtue? If the rights and duties of Christian magistrates and subjects are disputed, should they not explain them, show their nature, ends, limitations, and restrictions, how much soever it may move the gall of [their opponents]?

—John Adams, *Novanglus*, Feb. 1775

January 18

Can the liberties of a nation be thought secure when we have removed their only firm basis, a conviction in the minds of the people that these liberties are the gift of God? That they are not to be violated but with his wrath? Indeed I tremble for my country when I reflect that God is just: that his justice cannot sleep forever.

—Thomas Jefferson, *Notes on the State of Virginia,* 1781

January 19

But where, says some, is the king of America? I'll tell you, Friend, he reigns above. . . . Let a day be solemnly set apart for proclaiming the charter [a proposed constitution of America]; let it be brought forth placed on the divine law, the word of God; let a crown be placed thereon, by which the world may know, that so far as we approve as monarchy, that in America THE LAW IS KING. For as in absolute governments the king is law, so in free countries the law *ought* to be king; and there ought to be no other.

—Thomas Paine, *Common Sense,* 1776

January 20

Observe good faith and justice towards all nations; cultivate peace and harmony with all. Religion and morality enjoin this conduct; and can it be, that good policy does not equally enjoin it? It will be worthy of a free, enlightened, and, at no distant period, a great nation, to give to mankind the magnanimous and too novel example of a people always guided by an exalted justice and benevolence. Who can doubt, that, in the course of time and things, the fruits of such a plan would richly repay any temporary advantages, which might be lost by a steady adherence to it? Can it be, that Providence has not connected the permanent felicity of a nation with its virtue? The experiment, at least, is recommended by every sentiment which ennobles human nature.

—George Washington, Farewell Address, Sept. 19, 1796

January 21

The true key for the construction of everything doubtful in a law is the intention of the law-makers. This is most safely gathered from the words, but may be sought also in extraneous circumstances, provided they do not contradict the express words of the law. . . . I am for going substantially to the object of the law, and no further.

—Thomas Jefferson to Albert Gallatin, May 20, 1808

January 22

The real wonder is that so many difficulties should have been surmounted, and surmounted with a unanimity almost as unprecedented as it must have been unexpected. It is impossible for any man of candor to reflect on this circumstance without partaking of the astonishment. It is impossible for the man of pious reflection not to perceive in it a finger of that Almighty hand which has been so frequently and signally extended to our relief in the critical stages of the revolution.

—James Madison, Federalist No. 37, 1788

January 23

It has long . . . been my opinion, and I have never shrunk from its expression . . . that the germ of dissolution of our federal government is in the constitution of the federal judiciary; an irresponsible body (for impeachment is scarcely a scare-crow), working like gravity by night and by day, gaining a little today and a little tomorrow, and advancing its noiseless step like a thief, over the field of jurisdiction, until all shall be usurped from the states, and the government of all be consolidated into one.

—Thomas Jefferson to Charles Hammond,
Aug. 18, 1821

January 24

Those who expect to reap the blessings of freedom, must, like men, undergo the fatigues of supporting it. . . . It is not a field of a few acres of ground, but a cause, that we are defending, and whether we defeat the enemy in one battle, or by degrees, the consequences will be the same. . . .

Men who are sincere in defending their freedom will always feel concern at every circumstance which seems to make against them; it is the natural and honest consequence of all affectionate attachments, and the want of it is a vice. But the dejection lasts only for a moment; they soon rise out of it with additional vigor; the glow of hope, courage and fortitude, will, in a little time, supply the place of every inferior passion, and kindle the whole heart into heroism.

—Thomas Paine, *American Crisis*, no, 4,
Sept. 11, 1777

January 25

I am for doing good to the poor, but I differ in opinion of the means. I think the best way of doing good to the poor, is not making them easy in poverty, but leading or driving them out of it. In my youth I traveled much, and I observed in different countries, that the more public provisions were made for the poor, the less they provided for themselves, and of course became poorer. And, on the contrary, the less was done for them, the more they did for themselves, and became richer.

—Benjamin Franklin, "On the Price of Corn and Management of the Poor," Nov. 1766

January 26

Now to what higher object, to what greater character, can any mortal aspire than to be possessed of all this knowledge, well digested and ready at command, to assist the feeble and friendless, to discountenance the haughty and lawless, to procure redress to wrongs, the advancement of rights, to assert and maintain liberty and virtue to discourage and abolish tyranny and vice.

—John Adams to Jonathan Sewall, Oct. 1759

January 27

Mr. President: I confess that there are several parts of this constitution which I do not at present approve, but I am not sure I shall never approve them: For having lived long, I have experienced many instances of being obliged by better information, or fuller consideration, to change opinions even on important subjects, which

I once thought right, but found to be otherwise. It is therefore that the older I grow, the more apt I am to doubt my own judgment, and to pay more respect to the judgment of others.

—Benjamin Franklin, Constitutional Convention,
Sept. 17, 1787

January 28

We have not yet so far perfected our constitutions as to venture to make them unchangeable. But still, in their present state, we consider them not otherwise changeable than by the authority of the people, on a special election of representatives for that purpose expressly: they are until then the *lex legum* [law of laws]. . . . Nothing then is unchangeable but the inherent and unalienable rights of man.

—Thomas Jefferson to John Cartwright,
June 5, 1824

January 29

Of all the dispositions and habits which lead to political prosperity, religion and morality are indispensable supports. In vain would that man claim the tribute of patriotism, who should labor to subvert these great pillars of human happiness, these firmest props of the duties of men and citizens. The mere politician, equally with the pious man, ought to respect and cherish them. A volume could not trace all their connections with private and public felicity.

—George Washington, Farewell Address,
Sept. 19, 1796

January 30

I give my signature to many bills with which my judgment is at variance. . . . From the nature of the Constitution, I must approve all parts of a bill, or reject it in total. To do the latter can only be justified upon the clear and obvious grounds of propriety; and I never had such confidence in my own faculty of judging as to be over tenacious of the opinions I may have imbibed in doubtful cases.

—George Washington to Edmund Pendleton,
Sept. 23, 1793

January 31

I know no safe depository of the ultimate powers of the society but the people themselves; and if we think them not enlightened enough to exercise their control with a wholesome discretion, the remedy is not to take it from them, but to inform their discretion by education. This is the true corrective of abuses of constitutional power.

—Thomas Jefferson to William Charles Jarvis,
Sept. 28, 1820

FEBRUARY

February 1

Property must be secured, or liberty cannot exist. But if unlimited or unbalanced power of disposing property be put into the hands of those who have no property, France will find, as we have found, the lamb committed to the custody of the wolf. In such a case, all the pathetic exhortations and addresses of the national assembly to the people, to respect property, will be regarded no more than the warbles of the songsters of the forest.

—John Adams, *Discourses on Davila,* 1790

February 2

Reading, reflection and time have convinced me that the interests of society require the observation of those moral precepts . . . in which all religions agree. . . . The practice of morality being necessary for the well-being of society, [the Creator] has taken care to impress its precepts so indelibly on our hearts that they shall not be effaced by the subtleties of our brain.

—Thomas Jefferson to James Fishback, Sept. 27, 1809

February 3

O ye that love mankind! Ye that dare oppose, not only the tyranny, but the tyrant, stand forth! Every spot of the old world is overrun with oppression. Freedom hath been hunted round the globe. Asia, and Africa, have long expelled her—Europe regards her like a stranger, and England hath given her warning to depart. O! receive the fugitive, and prepare in time an asylum for mankind.

—Thomas Paine, *Common Sense*, 1776

February 4

If it be asked, what is to restrain the House of Representatives from making legal discriminations in favor of themselves and a particular class of the society? I answer: the genius of the whole system; the nature of just and constitutional laws; and above all, the vigilant and manly spirit which actuates the people of America—a spirit which nourishes freedom, and in return is nourished by it. If this spirit shall ever be so far debased as to tolerate a law not obligatory on the legislature, as well as on the people, the people will be prepared to tolerate anything but liberty.

—James Madison, Federalist, No. 57, 1788

February 5

Public virtue cannot exist in a nation without private, and public virtue is the only foundation of republics. There must be a positive passion for the public good, the public interest, honor, power and glory, established in the minds of the people, or there can be no republican government, nor any real liberty: and this public passion must be superior to all private passions. Men must be ready, they must pride themselves and be happy to sacrifice their private pleasures, passions and interests, nay, their private friendships and dearest connections, when they stand in competition with the rights of society.

—John Adams to Mercy Warren, Apr. 16, 1776

February 6

I wish it were possible to obtain a single amendment to our Constitution. I would be willing to depend on that alone for the reduction of the administration of our government to the genuine principles of its Constitution; I mean an additional article, taking from the federal government the power of borrowing.

—Thomas Jefferson to John Taylor, Nov. 26, 1798

February 7

The truth is, all might be free, if they valued freedom and defended it as they ought. . . . If, therefore, a people will not be free, if they have not virtue enough to maintain their liberty against a presumptuous invader, they deserve no pity, and are to be treated with contempt and ignominy.

It behooves us . . . to awake, and advert to the danger we are in. The tragedy of American freedom, it is to be feared, is nearly completed. A tyranny seems to be at the very door. . . .

Our enemies would fain have us lie down on the bed of sloth and security, and persuade ourselves that there is no danger. They are daily administering the opiate with multiplied arts and delusions, and I am sorry to observe that the gilded pill is so alluring to some who call themselves the friends of liberty.

—Samuel Adams, writing as Candidus,
Boston Gazette, Oct. 14, 1771

February 8

Nothing is more fallacious than to expect to produce any valuable or permanent results, in political projects, by relying merely on the reason of men. Men are rather reasoning than reasonable animals for the most part governed by the impulse of passion. This is a truth well understood by our adversaries who have practiced upon it with no small benefit to their cause. For at the very moment they are eulogizing the reason of men and professing to appeal only to that faculty, they are courting the strongest and most active passion of the human heart—*vanity!*

—Alexander Hamilton to James A. Bayard,
Apr. 16, 1802

February 9

The aim of every political Constitution is, or ought to be, first to obtain for rulers men who possess most wisdom to discern, and most virtue to pursue, the common good of society; and in the next place, to take the most effectual precautions for keeping them virtuous whilst they continue to hold their public trust. . . . The most effectual one, is such a limitation of the term of appointments as will maintain a proper responsibility to the people.

—James Madison, Federalist No. 57, 1788

February 10

The system of the general government is to seize all doubtful ground. We [the states] must join in the scramble or get nothing. Where first occupancy is to give a right, he who lies still loses all. . . . It is of immense consequence that the states retain as complete authority as possible over their own citizens.

—Thomas Jefferson to James Monroe, Sept. 7, 1797

February 11

The unity of government which constitutes you one people is also now dear to you. It is justly so, for it is a main pillar in the edifice of your real independence, the support of your tranquility at home, your peace abroad; of your safety; of your prosperity; of that very liberty which you so highly prize. But . . . as this is the point in your political fortress against which the batteries of internal and external enemies will be most constantly and actively (though often covertly and insidiously) directed, it is of infinite moment that you should properly estimate the immense value of your national union to your collective and individual happiness; that you should cherish a cordial, habitual, and immovable attachment to it; accustoming yourselves to think and speak of it as of the palladium of your political safety and prosperity; watching for its preservation with jealous anxiety; . . . and indignantly frowning upon the first dawning of every attempt to alienate any portion of our country from the rest, or to enfeeble the sacred ties which now link together the various parts.

—George Washington, Farewell Address,
Sept. 19, 1796

February 12

As there is a degree of depravity in mankind which requires a certain degree of circumspection and distrust: So
there are other qualities in human nature, which justify
a certain portion of esteem and confidence. Republican
government presupposes the existence of these qualities
in a higher degree than any other form.

—James Madison, Federalist No. 55, 1788

February 13

It is a wise rule and should be fundamental in a government disposed to cherish its credit, and at the same time
to restrain the use of it within the limits of its faculties,
never to borrow a dollar without laying a tax in the same
instant for paying the interest annually, and the principal
within a given term; and to consider that tax as pledged
to the creditors on the public faith.

—Thomas Jefferson to John Wayles Eppes,
June 24, 1813

February 14

To exclude foreign intrigues and foreign partialities, so
degrading to all countries and so baneful to free ones;
to foster a spirit of independence too just to invade the
rights of others, too proud to surrender our own, too
liberal to indulge unworthy prejudices ourselves and
too elevated not to look down upon them in others; to
hold the union of the states on the basis of their peace
and happiness; to support the Constitution, which is the
cement of the union, as well in its limitations as in its au-

thorities; to respect the rights and authorities reserved to the states and to the people as equally incorporated with and essential to the success of the general system; . . . to preserve in their full energy the other salutary provisions in behalf of private and personal rights . . . —as far as sentiments and intentions such as these can aid the fulfillment of my duty, they will be a resource which cannot fail me.

—James Madison, First Inaugural Address, Mar. 4, 1809

February 15

We have no government armed with power capable of contending with human passions unbridled by morality and religion. Avarice, ambition, revenge, or gallantry, would break the strongest cords of our Constitution as a whale goes through a net. Our Constitution was made only for a moral and religious people. It is wholly inadequate to the government of any other.

—John Adams, Address to the Military, Oct. 11, 1798

February 16

Those who live under arbitrary power do never the less approve of liberty, and wish for it. . . . It is a common observation here [Paris] that our cause is the cause of all mankind, and that we are fighting for their liberty in defending our own. Tis a glorious task assigned us by Providence; which has I trust given us spirit and virtue equal to it, and will at last crown it with success.

—Benjamin Franklin to Samuel Cooper, May 1, 1777

February 17

[I hope] that the foundations of our national policy will
be laid in the pure and immutable principles of private
morality, and the preeminence of free government [will]
be exemplified by all the attributes which can win the
affections of its citizens, and command the respect of
the world.

—George Washington, First Inaugural Address,
Apr. 30, 1789

February 18

Children should be educated and instructed in the principles of freedom. Aristotle speaks plainly to this purpose,
saying, "that the institution of youth should be accommo-
dated to that form of government under which they live;
forasmuch as it makes exceedingly for the preservation
of the present government, whatsoever it be."

—John Adams, *A Defence of the Constitutions
of Government,* 1787

February 19

But with respect to future debts; would it not be wise and
just for that nation [France] to declare in the constitution
they are forming that neither the legislature, nor the
nation itself can validly contract more debt than they
may pay within their own age, or within the term of
19 years?

—Thomas Jefferson to James Madison,
Sept. 6, 1789

February 20

It is the greatest absurdity to suppose it in the power of one, or of any number of men, at the entering into society to renounce their essential natural rights, or the means of preserving those rights, when the grand end of civil government, from the very nature of its institution, is for the support, protection, and defense of those very rights; the principal of which, as is before observed, are life, liberty, and property. If men, through fear, fraud, or mistake, should *in terms* renounce or give up an essential natural right, the eternal law of reason and the grand end of society would absolutely vacate such renunciation. The right of freedom being *the gift* of God Almighty, it is not in the power of man to alienate this gift and voluntarily become a slave.

—Samuel Adams, "Rights of the Colonists," 1772

February 21

We have the most sensible concern for the poor distressed inhabitants of the frontiers [who were engaged in hostilities with the Delawares and the Shawnees]. We have taken every step in our power, consistent with the just rights of the freemen of Pennsylvania, for their relief, and we have reason to believe, that in the midst of their distresses they themselves do not wish us to go farther. Those who would give up essential liberty, to purchase a little temporary safety, deserve neither liberty nor safety.

—Benjamin Franklin, written for the Pennsylvania Assembly in its *Reply to the Governor*, Nov. 11, 1755

February 22

For the same reason that the members of the state legislatures will be unlikely to attach themselves sufficiently to national objects, the members of the federal legislature will be likely to attach themselves too much to local objects. . . . The new federal government will . . . be disinclined to invade the rights of the individual states, or the prerogatives of their governments.

—James Madison, Federalist No. 46, 1788

February 23

Freedom had been hunted round the globe; reason was considered as rebellion; and the slavery of fear had made men afraid to think. But such is the irresistible nature of truth, that all it asks—and all it wants—is the liberty of appearing. The sun needs no inscription to distinguish him from darkness; and no sooner did the American governments display themselves to the world, than despotism felt a shock and man began to contemplate redress.

—Thomas Paine, *Rights of Man*, 1791

February 24

It should be the highest ambition of every American to extend his views beyond himself, and to bear in mind that his conduct will not only affect himself, his country, and his immediate posterity; but that its influence may be co-extensive with the world, and stamp political happiness or misery on ages yet unborn.

—George Washington to the Legislature
of Pennsylvania, Sept. 5, 1789

February 25

When a people is corrupted, the press may be made an engine to complete their ruin. . . . Liberty can no more exist without virtue and independence, than the body can live and move without a soul. When these are gone, . . . all other forms of the constitution may remain; but if you look for liberty, you will grope in vain, and the freedom of the press, instead of promoting the cause of liberty, will but hasten its destruction.

—John Adams, *Novanglus*, Feb. 1775

February 26

The people . . . are the ultimate guardians of their own liberty. . . . History by apprising them of the past will enable them to judge of the future; it will avail them of the experience of other times and other nations; it will qualify them as judges of the actions and designs of men; it will enable them to know ambition under every disguise it may assume; and knowing it, to defeat its views.

—Thomas Jefferson, *Notes on the State of Virginia,* 1781

February 27

Whatever may be the judgment pronounced on the competency of the architects of the Constitution, or whatever may be the destiny of the edifice prepared by them, I feel it a duty to express my profound and solemn conviction . . . that there never was an assembly of men, charged with a great and arduous trust, who were more pure in

their motives, or more exclusively or anxiously devoted
to the object committed to them . . . [to] best secure the
permanent liberty and happiness of their country.

—James Madison, preface to the Debates
of the Convention, circa 1830 to 1836

February 28

I am sure that there never was a people who had more
reason to acknowledge a divine interposition in their
affairs than those of the United States; and I should be
pained to believe that they have forgotten that agency
which was so often manifested during the Revolution, or
that they failed to consider the omnipotence of that God
who is alone able to protect them. He must be worse than
an infidel that lacks faith, and more than wicked that has
not gratitude enough to acknowledge his obligations.

—George Washington to John Armstrong,
Mar. 11, 1782

MARCH

March 1

Resolved . . . that it would be a dangerous delusion were a confidence in the men of our choice to silence our fears for the safety of our rights: that confidence is everywhere the parent of despotism—free government is founded in jealousy, and not in confidence; it is jealousy and not confidence which prescribes limited constitutions, to bind down those whom we are obliged to trust with power: that our Constitution has accordingly fixed the limits to which, and no further, our confidence may go.

—Thomas Jefferson, The Virginia and
Kentucky Resolutions, 1798

March 2

I never doubted . . . the existence of the Deity; that he made the world, and governed it by his Providence; that the most acceptable service of God was the doing good to man; that our souls are immortal; and that all crime will be punished, and virtue rewarded either here or hereafter. These I esteemed the essentials of every religion.

—Benjamin Franklin, *Autobiography*, 1790

March 3

I go further, and affirm that bills of rights, in the sense and to the extent in which they are contended for, are not only unnecessary in the proposed Constitution, but would even be dangerous. They would contain various exceptions to powers not granted; and on this very account, would afford a colorable pretext to claim more than were granted. For why declare that things shall not be done which there is no power to do?

—Alexander Hamilton, Federalist No. 84, 1788

March 4

Whereas it appeareth that however certain forms of government are better calculated than others to protect individuals in the free exercise of their natural rights, and are at the same time themselves better guarded against degeneracy, yet experience hath shewn, that even under the best forms, those entrusted with power have, in time, and by slow operations, perverted it into tyranny; and it is believed that the most effectual means of preventing this would be, to illuminate, as far as practicable, the minds of the people at large, . . . whence it becomes expedient for promoting the public happiness that those persons, whom nature hath endowed with genius and virtue, should be rendered by liberal education worthy to receive, and able to guard the sacred deposit of the rights and liberties of their fellow citizens, and that they should be called to that charge without regard to wealth, birth or accidental condition of circumstance.

—Thomas Jefferson, "A Bill for the More General
Diffusion of Knowledge," 1778

March 5

Of all the enemies to public liberty war is, perhaps, the most to be dreaded, because it comprises and develops the germ of every other. War is the parent of armies; from these proceed debts and taxes; and armies, and debts, and taxes are the known instruments for bringing the many under the domination of the few. In war, too, the discretionary power of the executive is extended; its influence in dealing out offices, honors, and emoluments is multiplied; and all the means of seducing the minds, are added to those of subduing the force, of the people. The same malignant aspect in republicanism may be traced in the inequality of fortunes, and the opportunities of fraud, growing out of a state of war, and in the degeneracy of manners and of morals engendered by both. No nation could preserve its freedom in the midst of continual warfare.

—James Madison, "Political Observations,"
Apr. 1795

March 6

The Constitution on which our union rests, shall be administered by me [as president] according to the safe and honest meaning contemplated by the plain understanding of the people of the United States at the time of its adoption—a meaning to be found in the explanations of those who advocated, not those who opposed it, and who opposed it merely lest the construction should be applied which they denounced as possible.

—Thomas Jefferson to Messrs. Eddy, Russel, Thurber,
Wheaton and Smith, Mar. 27, 1801

March 7

All of us who were engaged in the struggle must have observed frequent instances of superintending providence in our favor. To that kind providence we owe this happy opportunity of consulting in peace on the means of establishing our future national felicity. And have we now forgotten that powerful friend? Or do we imagine that we no longer need his assistance? . . . .

I therefore beg leave to move—that henceforth prayers imploring the assistance of Heaven, and its blessing on our deliberations, be held in this Assembly every morning before we proceed to business, and that one or more of the clergy of this city be requested to officiate in that service.

—Benjamin Franklin, Constitutional Convention,
June 28, 1787

March 8

The science of government it is my duty to study, more than all other sciences; the arts of legislation and administration and negotiation ought to take the place of, indeed exclude, in a manner, all other arts. I must study politics and war, that my sons may have liberty to study mathematics and philosophy. My sons ought to study mathematics and philosophy, geography, natural history and naval architecture, navigation, commerce and agriculture in order to give their children a right to study painting, poetry, music, architecture, statuary, tapestry and porcelain.

—John Adams to Abigail Adams, May 12, 1780

March 9

Nations pay little regard to rules and maxims calculated in their very nature to run counter to the necessities of society. Wise politicians will be cautious about fettering the government with restrictions that cannot be observed, because they know that every breach of the fundamental laws, though dictated by necessity, impairs that sacred reverence which ought to be maintained in the breast of rulers towards the constitution of a country, and forms a precedent for other breaches where the same plea of necessity does not exist at all, or is less urgent and palpable.

—Alexander Hamilton, Federalist No. 25, 1787

March 10

Freedom of thought and the right of private judgment, in matters of conscience, driven from every other corner of the earth, direct their course to this happy country as their last asylum. Let us cherish the noble guests, and shelter them under the wings of a universal toleration! Be this the seat of unbounded religious freedom. She will bring with her in her train, industry, wisdom, and commerce. She thrives most when left to shoot forth in her natural luxuriance. . . .

Thus, by the beneficence of Providence, we shall behold our empire arising, . . . giving full scope to the exercise of those faculties and rights which most ennoble our species.

—Samuel Adams, speech, Pennsylvania State House, Philadelphia, Aug. 1, 1776

March 11

It will be equally forgotten that the vigor of government
is essential to the security of liberty; that, in the contem-
plation of a sound and well-informed judgment, their
interest can never be separated; and that a dangerous
ambition more often lurks behind the specious mask of
zeal for the rights of the people than under the forbidden
appearance of zeal for the firmness and efficiency of
government. History will teach us that the former has
been found a much more certain road to the introduction
of despotism than the latter, and that of those men who
have overturned the liberties of republics, the greatest
number have begun their career by paying an obsequious
court to the people; commencing demagogues, and end-
ing tyrants.

—Alexander Hamilton, Federalist, No. 1, 1787

March 12

Repeal that [welfare] law, and you will soon see a change
in their manners. St. Monday and St. Tuesday, will soon
cease to be holidays. Six days shalt thou labor, though
one of the old commandments, long treated as out of
date, will again be looked upon as a respectable pre-
cept; industry will increase, and with it plenty among
the lower people; their circumstances will mend, and
more will be done for their happiness by inuring them to
provide for themselves, than could be done by dividing
all your estates among them.

—Benjamin Franklin to Peter Collinson,
May 9, 1753

March 13

Harmony, liberal intercourse with all nations, are recommended by policy, humanity, and interest. But . . . it is folly in one nation to look for disinterested favors from another; that it must pay with a portion of its independence for whatever it may accept under that character; that by such acceptance, it may place itself in the condition of having given equivalents for nominal favors and yet of being reproached with ingratitude for not giving more. There can be no greater error than to expect, or calculate upon real favors from nation to nation. 'Tis an illusion which experience must cure, which a just pride ought to discard.

—George Washington, Farewell Address,
Sept. 19, 1796

March 14

The mutability in the public councils arising from a rapid succession of new members, . . . points out . . . the necessity of some stable institution in the government [i.e., the Senate]. . . . The internal effects of a mutable policy are still more calamitous. It poisons the blessing of liberty itself. It will be of little avail to the people, that the laws are made by men of their own choice, if the laws be so voluminous that they cannot be read, or so incoherent that they cannot be understood; if they be repealed or revised before they are promulgated, or undergo such incessant changes that no man, who knows what the law is to-day, can guess what it will be tomorrow. Law is defined to be a rule of action; but how can that be a rule, which is little known, and less fixed?

—James Madison, Federalist No. 62, 1788

March 15

If it had not been for the justice of our cause, and the consequent interposition of Providence, in which we had faith, we must have been ruined. If had ever before been an atheist, I should now have been convinced of the being and government of a Deity! It is He who abases the proud and favors the humble. May we never forget His goodness to us, and may our future conduct manifest our gratitude.

—Benjamin Franklin to William Strahan,
Aug. 19, 1784

March 16

[In] the first stage of this education . . . the first elements of morality too may be instilled into their minds; such as, when further developed as their judgments advance in strength, may teach them how to work out their own greatest happiness, by shewing them that it does not depend on the condition of life in which chance has placed them, but is always the result of a good conscience, good health, occupation, and freedom in all just pursuits.

—Thomas Jefferson, *Notes on the State of Virginia*, 1785

March 17

The people . . . have a right, an indisputable, unalienable, indefeasible, divine right to that most dreaded and envied kind of knowledge, I mean, of the characters and conduct of their rulers. Rulers are no more than attorneys, agents, and trustees, of the people; and if the cause, the interest, and trust, is insidiously betrayed, or wantonly trifled away, the people have a right to revoke the authority that they themselves have deputed, and to constitute other and better agents, attorneys and trustees.

—John Adams, *A Dissertation on the Canon and Feudal Law,* 1765

March 18

In reality there is perhaps no one of our natural passions so hard to subdue as pride. Disguise it, struggle with it, beat it down, stifle it, mortify it as much as one pleases, it is still alive, and will every now and then peep out and show itself. You see it perhaps often in this history. For even if I could conceive that I had completely overcome it, I should probably be proud of my humility.

—Benjamin Franklin, *Autobiography,* 1771

March 19

There are certain social principles in human nature, from which we may draw the most solid conclusions with respect to the conduct of individuals and of communities. We love our families more than our neighbors; we love our neighbors more than our countrymen in general. The human affections, like solar heat, lose their intensity as they depart from the center. . . . On these principles, the attachment of the individual will be first and forever secured by the state governments. They will be a mutual protection and support.

—Alexander Hamilton, New York Ratifying Convention, June 1788

March 20

The great secret of succeeding in conversation is to admire little, to hear much; always to distrust our own
reason, and sometimes that of our friends; never to pre-
tend to wit, but to make that of others appear as much
as possibly we can; to hearken to what is said, and to
answer to the purpose.

—Benjamin Franklin, "Miscellaneous Observations,"
1728

March 21

As to my sentiments with respect to the merits of the
new Constitution, I will disclose them without reserve
(although by passing through the post offices they should
become known to all the world). . . . It appears to me,
then, little short of a miracle, that the delegates from
so many different states . . . should unite in forming a
system of national government, so little liable to well-
founded objections.

—George Washington to Marquis de Lafayette,
Feb. 7, 1788

March 22

To judge from the conduct of the opposite parties, we
shall be led to conclude that they will mutually hope
to evince the justness of their opinions, and to increase
the number of their converts by the loudness of their
declamations and the bitterness of their invectives. An
enlightened zeal for the energy and efficiency of government will be stigmatized as the offspring of a temper

fond of despotic power and hostile to the principles of liberty. An over-scrupulous jealousy of danger to the rights of the people, which is more commonly the fault of the head than of the heart, will be represented as mere pretense and artifice, the stale bait for popularity at the expense of the public good.

—Alexander Hamilton, Federalist No. 1, 1787

March 23

Cities may be rebuilt, and a people reduced to poverty, may acquire fresh property: But a constitution of government once changed from freedom, can never be restored. Liberty once lost is lost forever. When the people once surrendered their share in the legislature, and their right of defending the limitations upon the government, and of resisting every encroachment upon them, they can never regain it.

—John Adams to Abigail Adams, July 7, 1775

March 24

It is the nature and intention of a constitution to prevent governing by party, by establishing a common principle that shall limit and control the power and impulse of party, and that says to all parties, thus far shalt thou go and no further. But in the absence of a constitution, men look entirely to party; and instead of principle governing party, party governs principle.

—Thomas Paine, *First Principles of Government,* 1795

March 25

We have therefore to resolve to conquer or die: Our own country's honor, all call upon us for vigorous and manly exertion, and if we now shamefully fail, we shall become infamous to the whole world. Let us therefore rely upon the goodness of the cause, and the aid of the supreme Being, in whose hands victory is, to animate and encourage us to great and noble actions.

—George Washington, General Orders,
July 2, 1776

March 26

Give up money, give up fame, give up science, give the earth itself and all it contains rather than do an immoral act. And never suppose that in any possible situation, or under any circumstances, it is best for you to do a dishonorable thing, however slightly so it may appear to you. . . . From the practice of the purest virtue, you may be assured you will derive the most sublime comforts in every moment of life, and in the moment of death.

—Thomas Jefferson to his nephew Peter Carr,
Aug. 19, 1785

March 27

Gentlemen indulge too many unreasonable apprehensions of danger to the state governments [if the new Constitution is ratified]. They seem to suppose that the moment you put men into the national council, they become corrupt and tyrannical. . . . While the Constitution continues to be read, and its principles known, the states, must, by every rational man, be considered as essential component parts of the union; and therefore the idea of sacrificing the former to the latter is totally inadmissible.

—Alexander Hamilton, New York Ratifying Convention, June 24, 1788

March 28

When all government, domestic and foreign, in little as in great things, shall be drawn to Washington as the center of all power, it will render powerless the checks provided of one government on another and will become as venal and oppressive as the government from which we separated. . . . If the states look with apathy on this silent descent of their government into the gulf which is to swallow all, we have only to weep over the human character formed uncontrollable but by a rod of iron, and the blasphemers of man, as incapable of self-government, become his true historians.

—Thomas Jefferson to Charles Hammond, Aug. 18, 1821

March 29

When you assemble a number of men to have the advantage of their joint wisdom, you inevitably assemble with those men, all their prejudices, their passions, their errors of opinion, their local interests, and their selfish views. From such an assembly can a perfect production be expected? It therefore astonishes me, Sir, to find this system approaching so near to perfection as it does.

—Benjamin Franklin, Constitutional Convention, Sept. 17, 1787

March 30

I am well aware of the toil and blood and treasure that it will cost us to maintain this Declaration [of Independence], and support and defend these states. Yet through all the gloom I can see the rays of ravishing light and glory. I can see that the end is more than worth all the means. And that posterity will triumph in that day's transaction, even although we should rue it, which I trust in God we shall not.

—John Adams to Abigail Adams, July 3, 1776

March 31

Neither the wisest constitution nor the wisest laws will secure the liberty and happiness of a people whose manners are universally corrupt. He therefore is the truest friend to the liberty of his country who tries most to promote its virtue, and who, so far as his power and influence extend, will not suffer a man to be chosen into any office of power and trust who is not a wise and virtuous man. We must not conclude merely upon a man's haranguing upon liberty, and using the charming sound, that he is fit to be trusted with the liberties of his country. It is not unfrequent to hear men declaim loudly upon liberty, who, if we may judge by the whole tenor of their actions, mean nothing else by it *but their own liberty*. . . . The sum of all is, if we would most truly enjoy this gift of Heaven, let us become a virtuous people.

—Samuel Adams, essay in *The Advertiser,* 1748

APRIL

April 1

Natural liberty is a gift of the beneficent Creator, to the whole human race; and that civil liberty is founded in that; and cannot be wrested from any people, without the most manifest violation of justice. *Civil liberty is only natural liberty, modified and secured by the sanctions of civil society.* It is not a thing, in its own nature, precarious and dependent on human will and caprice; but it is conformable to the constitution of man, as well as necessary to the *well-being* of society.

—Alexander Hamilton, "The Farmer Refuted,"
Feb. 23, 1775

April 2

On every question of construction [of the Constitution], carry ourselves back to the time when the Constitution was adopted, recollect the spirit manifested in the debates, and instead of trying what meaning may be squeezed out of the text, or invented against it, conform to the probable one in which it was passed.

—Thomas Jefferson to William Johnson,
June 12, 1823

April 3

Wherever the real power in a government lies, there is the danger of oppression. In our governments, the real power lies in the majority of the community, and the invasion of private rights is chiefly to be apprehended, not from the acts of government contrary to the sense of its constituents, but from acts in which the government is the mere instrument of the major number of the constituents.

—James Madison to Thomas Jefferson, Oct. 17, 1788

April 4

It is an unquestionable truth, that the body of the people in every country desire sincerely its prosperity. But it is equally unquestionable that they do not possess the discernment and stability necessary for systematic government. To deny that they are frequently led into the grossest of errors, by misinformation and passion, would be a flattery which their own good sense must despise.

—Alexander Hamilton, New York Ratifying
Convention, June 1788

April 5

I go on this great republican principle, that the people will have virtue and intelligence to select men of virtue and wisdom. Is there no virtue among us? If there be not, we are in a wretched situation. No theoretical checks, no form of government, can render us secure. To suppose that any form of government will secure liberty or happiness without any virtue in the people, is a chimerical idea. If there be sufficient virtue and intelligence in the community, it will be exercised in the selection of these men; so that we do not depend on their virtue, or put confidence in our rulers, but in the people who are to choose them.

—James Madison, Virginia Ratifying Convention,
June 20, 1788

April 6

Among the natural rights of the colonists are these: first, a right to life; second, to liberty; third, to property; together with the right to support and defend them in the best manner they can. These are evident branches of . . . the duty of self-preservation, commonly called the first law of nature. All men have a right to remain in a state of nature as long as they please; and in case of intolerable oppression, civil or religious, to leave the society they belong to, and enter into another. . . . Now what liberty can there be where property is taken away without consent?

—Samuel Adams, "The Rights of the Colonists,"
Nov. 1772

April 7

I now make it my earnest prayer, that God would have you, and the state over which you preside, in his holy protection; that he would incline the hearts of the citizens to cultivate a spirit of subordination and obedience to government; to entertain a brotherly affection and love for one another, for their fellow citizens of the United States at large; and, particularly, for their brethren who have served in the Geld; and finally, that he would most graciously be pleased to dispose us all to do justice, to love mercy, and to demean ourselves with that charity, humility, and pacific temper of the mind, which were the characteristics of the divine Author of our blessed religion; without an humble imitation of whose example, in these things, we can never hope to be a happy nation.

—George Washington, circular letter of farewell to the Army, June 8, 1783

April 8

Safety from external danger is the most powerful director of national conduct. Even the ardent love of liberty will, after a time, give way to its dictates. The violent destruction of life and property incident to war, the continual effort and alarm attendant on a state of continual danger, will compel nations the most attached to liberty to resort for repose and security to institutions which have a tendency to destroy their civil and political rights. To be more safe, they at length become willing to run the risk of being less free.

—Alexander Hamilton, Federalist No. 8, 1787

April 9

I wish to preserve the line drawn by the federal constitution between the general and particular [state] governments as it stands at present, and to take every prudent means of preventing either from stepping over it. Though the experiment has not yet had a long enough course to shew us from which quarter encroachments are most to be feared, yet it is easy to foresee from the nature of things that the encroachments of the state governments will tend to an excess of liberty which will correct itself . . . while those of the general government will tend to monarchy, which will fortify itself from day to day, instead of working its own cure, as all experience shews. I would rather be exposed to the inconveniencies attending too much liberty than those attending too small a degree of it. Then it is important to strengthen the state governments.

—Thomas Jefferson to Archibald Stewart,
Dec. 23, 1791

April 10

'Tis impossible to judge with much precision of the true motives and qualities of human actions, or of the propriety of rules contrived to govern them, without considering with like attention, all the passions, appetites, affections in nature from which they flow. An intimate knowledge therefore of the intellectual and moral world is the sole foundation on which a stable structure of knowledge can be erected.

—John Adams to Jonathan Sewall, Oct. 1759

April 11

The Constitution ought to be the standard of construction for the laws, and that wherever there is an evident opposition, the laws ought to give place to the Constitution. But this doctrine is not deducible from any circumstance peculiar to the plan of convention, but from the general theory of a limited Constitution.

—Alexander Hamilton, Federalist No. 81, 1788

April 12

The elective franchise, if guarded as the act of our safety, will peaceably dissipate all combinations to subvert a Constitution dictated by the wisdom, and resting on the will of the people. That will is the only legitimate foundation of any government, and to protect its free expression should be our first object. I offer my sincere prayers to the Supreme Ruler of the Universe, that He may long preserve our country in freedom and prosperity.

—Thomas Jefferson to Benjamin Waring,
Mar. 23, 1801

April 13

The transcendent law of nature and of nature's God, . . . declares that the safety and happiness of society are the objects at which all political institutions aim, and to which all such institutions must be sacrificed.

—James Madison, Federalist No. 43, 1788

April 14

The judiciary of the United States is the subtle corps of sappers and miners constantly working under ground to undermine the foundations of our confederated fabric. They are construing our constitution from a coordination of a general and special government to a general and supreme one alone. This will lay all things at their feet. . . . Having found, from experience, that impeachment is an impracticable thing, a mere scarecrow, they consider themselves secure for life; they skulk from responsibility to public opinion, the only remaining hold on them. . . . An opinion is huddled up in conclave, perhaps by a majority of one, delivered as if unanimous, and with the silent acquiescence of lazy or timid associates, by a crafty chief judge, who sophisticates the law to his mind, by the turn of his own reasoning

—Thomas Jefferson to Thomas Ritchie,
Dec. 25, 1820

April 15

Men who are sincere in defending their freedom, will always feel concern at every circumstance which seems to make against them; it is the natural and honest consequence of all affectionate attachments, and the want of it is a vice. But the dejection lasts only for a moment; they soon rise out of it with additional vigor; the glow of hope, courage and fortitude, will, in a little time, supply the place of every inferior passion, and kindle the whole heart into heroism.

—Thomas Paine, *American Crisis,* no. 4, Sept. 1777

April 16

If men of wisdom and knowledge, of moderation and temperance, of patience, fortitude and perseverance, of sobriety and true republican simplicity of manners, of zeal for the honor of the Supreme Being and the welfare of the commonwealth; if men possessed of these other excellent qualities are chosen to fill the seats of government, we may expect that our affairs will rest on a solid and permanent foundation.

—Samuel Adams to Elbridge Gerry, Nov. 27, 1780

April 17

The law no passion can disturb. 'Tis void of desire and fear, lust and anger. 'Tis *mens sine affectu* [mind without passion], written reason, retaining some measure of the divine perfection. It does not enjoin that which pleases a weak, frail man, but, without any regard to persons, commands that which is good and punishes evil in all, whether rich or poor, high or low. 'Tis deaf, inexorable, inflexible. On the one hand it is inexorable to the cries and lamentations of the prisoners; on the other it is deaf, deaf as an adder, to the clamors of the populace.

—John Adams, Boston Massacre trial,
Oct.–Dec. 1770

April 18

The king and the parliament are quarrelling for the oyster. The shell will be left as heretofore to the people. This it is to have a government which can be felt; a government of energy. God send that our country may never have a government, which it can feel. This is the perfection of human society.

—Thomas Jefferson to Francis Hopkinson,
May 8, 1788

April 19

All speculative politicians will agree, that the happiness of society is the end of government, as all divines and moral philosophers will agree that the happiness of the individual is the end of man. . . . All sober inquirers after truth, ancient and modern, pagan and Christian, have declared that the happiness of man, as well as his dignity, consists in virtue. . . . If there is a form of government, then, whose principle and foundation is virtue, will not every sober man acknowledge it better calculated to promote the general happiness than any other form?

—John Adams, *Thoughts on Government*, 1776

April 20

The people cannot be all, and always, well informed. The part which is wrong will be discontented, in proportion to the importance of the facts they misconceive. If they remain quiet under such misconceptions, it is lethargy, the forerunner of death to the public liberty.

—Thomas Jefferson to William S. Smith, Nov. 13, 1787

April 21

It is to be remembered that the general government is not to be charged with the whole power of making and administering laws: its jurisdiction is limited to certain enumerated objects, which concern all the members of the republic, but which are not to be attained by the separate provisions of any.

—James Madison, Federalist No. 14, 1787

April 22

There are persons . . . who see not the full extent of the evil which threatens them; they solace themselves with hopes that the enemy, if he succeed, will be merciful.

It is the madness of folly, to expect mercy from those who have refused to do justice; and even mercy, where conquest is the object, is only a trick of war; the cunning of the fox is as murderous as the violence of the wolf, and we ought to guard equally against both.

—Thomas Paine, *American Crisis,* no. 1,
Dec. 23, 1776

April 23

The way to wealth, if you desire it, is as plain as the way to market. It depends chiefly on two words, industry and frugality; that is, waste neither time nor money, but make the best use of both. Without industry and frugality nothing will do, and with them everything. He that gets all he can honestly, and saves all he gets (necessary expenses excepted), will certainly become rich, if that Being who governs the world, to whom all should look for a blessing on their honest endeavors, doth not, in his wise providence, otherwise determine.

—Benjamin Franklin, "Advice to a Young Tradesman,"
July 21, 1748

April 24

There are two tyrants in human life who domineer in all nations, . . . as well as in our simple, youthful, and beloved United States of America. These two tyrants are fashion and party. They are sometimes at variance, and I know not whether their mutual hostility is not the only security of human happiness. But they are forever struggling for an alliance with each other; and, when they are united, truth, reason, honor, justice, gratitude, and humanity itself in combination are no match for the coalition. Upon the maturest reflection of a long experience, I am much inclined to believe that fashion is the worst of all tyrants, because he is the original source, cause, preserver, and supporter of all others.

—John Adams to Samuel B. Malcolm, Aug. 6, 1812

April 25

Peace or war will not always be left to our option. . . . To judge from the history of mankind, we shall be compelled to conclude that the fiery and destructive passions of war reign in the human breast with much more powerful sway than the mild and beneficent sentiments of peace; and that to model our political systems upon speculations of lasting tranquility would be to calculate on the weaker springs of human character.

—Alexander Hamilton, Federalist No. 34, 1788

April 26

It is never to be expected in a revolution that every man is to change his opinion at the same moment. There never yet was any truth or any principle so irresistibly obvious that all men believed it at once. Time and reason must cooperate with each other to the final establishment of any principle; and therefore those who may happen to be first convinced have not a right to persecute others, on whom conviction operates more slowly. The moral principle of revolutions is to instruct, not to destroy.

—Thomas Paine, *First Principles of Government*, 1795

April 27

As to the history of the revolution, my ideas may be peculiar, perhaps singular. What do we mean by the revolution? The war? That was no part of the revolution; it was only an effect and consequence of it. The revolution was in the minds of the people, and this was effected from 1760–1775, in the course of fifteen years, before a drop of blood was shed at Lexington.

—John Adams to Thomas Jefferson, Aug. 24, 1815

April 28

To preserve . . . independence, we must not let our rulers load us with perpetual debt. We must make our election between economy and liberty or profusion and servitude. If we run into such debt, as that we must be taxed in our meat and in our drink, in our necessaries and our comforts, in our labors and our amusements, for our calling and our creeds . . . [we will] have no time to think, no means of calling our mismanagers to account but be glad to obtain subsistence by hiring ourselves to rivet their chains on the necks of our fellow-sufferers. . . . And this is the tendency of all human governments. A departure from principle in one instance becomes a precedent for [another] . . . till the bulk of society is reduced to be mere automatons of misery. . . . And the fore-horse of this frightful team is public debt. Taxation follows that, and in its train wretchedness and oppression.

—Thomas Jefferson to H. Tompkinson
(aka Samuel Kercheval), July 12, 1816

April 29

Virtue, by the constitution of nature carries in general its own reward, and vice its own punishment, even in this world. But as many exceptions to this rule, take place upon earth, the joys of heaven are prepared, and the horrors of hell in a future state to render the moral government of the universe, perfect and complete. Human government is more or less perfect as it approaches nearer or diverges farther from the imitation of this perfect plan of divine and moral government. . . . But when a government becomes totally corrupted, the system of God Almighty in the government of the world and the rules of all good government upon earth will be reversed, and virtue, integrity and ability will become the objects of the malice, hatred and revenge of the men in power, and folly, vice, and villainy will be cherished and supported.

—John Adams, draft of a newspaper communication,
circa Aug. 1770

April 30

To take from one, because it is thought his own industry and that of his fathers has acquired too much, in order to spare to others, who, or whose fathers, have not exercised equal industry and skill, is to violate arbitrarily the first principle of association—the guarantee to everyone the free exercise of his industry and the fruits acquired by it.

—Thomas Jefferson to Joseph Milligan, Apr. 6, 1816

MAY

May 1

It is too probable that no plan we propose will be adopted. Perhaps another dreadful conflict is to be sustained. If, to please the people, we offer what we ourselves disprove, how can we afterwards defend our work? Let us raise a standard to which the wise and the honest can repair. The event is in the hand of God.

—George Washington, Constitutional Convention,
Mar. 25, 1787

May 2

Considering the general tendency to multiply offices and dependencies and to increase expense to the ultimate term of burden which the citizen can bear, it behooves us to avail ourselves of every occasion which presents itself for taking off the surcharge; that it never may be seen here that, after leaving to labor the smallest portion of its earnings on which it can subsist, government shall itself consume the whole residue of what it was instituted to guard.

—Thomas Jefferson, First State of the Union Address,
Dec. 8, 1801

May 3

Good constitutions are formed upon a comparison of
the liberty of the individual with the strength of government: If the tone of either be too high, the other will be
weakened too much. It is the happiest possible mode of
conciliating these objects, to institute one branch peculiarly endowed with sensibility, another with knowledge
and firmness. Through the opposition and mutual control of these bodies, the government will reach, in its
regular operations, the perfect balance between liberty
and power.

—Alexander Hamilton, New York Ratifying
Convention, June 25, 1788

May 4

We hold it for a fundamental and undeniable truth, "that
religion or the duty which we owe to our Creator and
the manner of discharging it, can be directed only by
reason and conviction, not by force or violence." The
religion then of every man must be left to the conviction
and conscience of every man; and it is the right of every
man to exercise it as these may dictate. This right is in
its nature an unalienable right. It is unalienable; because
the opinions of men, depending only on the evidence
contemplated by their own minds, cannot follow the
dictates of other men: It is unalienable also; because
what is here a right towards men, is a duty towards the
Creator.

—James Madison, "Memorial and Remonstrance
against Religious Assessments," June 20, 1785

May 5

Citizens by birth or choice of a common country, that country has a right to concentrate your affections. The name of American, which belongs to you, in your national capacity, must always exalt the just pride of patriotism, more than any appellation derived from local discriminations.

—George Washington, Farewell Address,
Sept. 19, 1796

May 6

It will not be denied that power is of an encroaching nature and that it ought to be effectually restrained from passing the limits assigned to it. After discriminating, therefore, in theory, the several classes of power, as they may in their nature be legislative, executive, or judiciary, the next and most difficult task is to provide some practical security for each, against the invasion of the others.

—James Madison, Federalist No. 48, 1788

May 7

When an instrument admits two constructions, the one safe, the other dangerous, the one precise, the other indefinite, I prefer that which is safe and precise. I had rather ask an enlargement of power from the nation [through amendment], where it is found necessary, than to assume it by a construction which would make our powers boundless. Our peculiar security is in the possession of a written Constitution. Let us not make it a blank paper by construction. . . . If it has bounds, they can

be no others than the definitions of the powers which
that instrument gives. It specifies and delineates the operations permitted to the federal government, and gives
all the powers necessary to carry these into execution.
Whatever of these enumerated objects is proper for a
law, Congress may make the law.

—Thomas Jefferson to Wilson Nicholas,
Sept. 7, 1803

May 8

Government is frequently and aptly classed under two
descriptions, a government of *force* and a government of
laws; the first is the definition of despotism—the last, of
liberty. But how can a government of laws exist where
the laws are disrespected and disobeyed? Government
supposes control. It is the *power* by which individuals in
society are kept from doing injury to each other and are
brought to cooperate to a common end. The instruments
by which it must act are either the *authority* of the laws
or *force*. If the first be destroyed, the last must be substi-
tuted; and where this becomes the ordinary instrument
of government there is an end to liberty.

—Alexander Hamilton, Tully, Aug. 28, 1794

May 9

Nip the shoots of arbitrary power in the bud, is the only
maxim which can ever preserve the liberties of any people. When the people give way, their deceivers, betrayers
and destroyers press upon them so fast that there is no
resisting afterwards. The nature of the encroachment
upon [the] American constitution is such, as to grow

every day more and more encroaching. Like a cancer, it eats faster and faster every hour. The revenue creates pensioners, and the pensioners urge for more revenue. The people grow less steady, spirited and virtuous, the seekers more numerous and more corrupt, and every day increases the circles of their dependents and expectants, until virtue, integrity, public spirit, simplicity, frugality, become the objects of ridicule and scorn, and vanity, luxury, foppery, selfishness, meanness, and downright venality, swallow up the whole society.

—John Adams, *Novanglus*, Feb. 1775

May 10

I believe the states can best govern our home concerns, and the general government our foreign ones. I wish, therefore, to see maintained that wholesome distribution of powers established by the constitution for the limitation of both; and never to see all offices transferred to Washington, where, further withdrawn from the eyes of the people, they may more secretly be bought and sold as at market.

—Thomas Jefferson to William Johnson,
June 12, 1823

May 11

Why has government been instituted at all? Because the passions of men will not conform to the dictates of reason and justice, without constraint. Has it been found that bodies of men act with more rectitude or greater disinterestedness than individuals? The contrary of this has been inferred by all accurate observers of the conduct of mankind; and the inference is founded upon obvious reasons. Regard to reputation has a less active influence, when the infamy of a bad action is to be divided among a number than when it is to fall singly upon one. A spirit of faction, which is apt to mingle its poison in the deliberations of all bodies of men, will often hurry the persons of whom they are composed into improprieties and excesses, for which they would blush in a private capacity.

—Alexander Hamilton, Federalist No. 15, 1787

May 12

With all these blessings, what more is necessary to make us a happy and prosperous people? Still one thing more, fellow-citizens—a wise and frugal government, which shall restrain men from injuring one another, shall leave them otherwise free to regulate their own pursuits of industry and improvement, and shall not take from the mouth of labor the bread it has earned. This is the sum of good government, and this is necessary to close the circle of our felicities.

—Thomas Jefferson, First Inaugural Address,
Mar. 4, 1801

May 13

I believe there is one Supreme most perfect Being. . . . I believe he is pleased and delights in the happiness of those he has created; and since without virtue man can have no happiness in this world, I firmly believe he delights to see me virtuous. . . . Let me then not fail to praise my God continually, for it is his due, and it is all I can return for his many favors and great goodness to me; and let me resolve to be virtuous, that I may be happy, that I may please Him, who is delighted to see me happy.

—Benjamin Franklin, "Articles of Belief and Acts of Religion," 1728

May 14

Society in every state is a blessing, but government even in its best state is but a necessary evil; in its worst state an intolerable one; for when we suffer, or are exposed to the same miseries *by a government*, which we might expect in a country *without government*, our calamity is heightened by reflecting that we furnish the means by which we suffer. Government, like dress, is the badge of lost innocence; the palaces of kings are built on the ruins of the bowers of paradise.

—Thomas Paine, *Common Sense,* 1776

May 15

I own myself the friend to a very free system of commerce, and hold it as a truth, that commercial shackles are generally unjust, oppressive and impolitic—it is also a truth, that if industry and labor are left to take their own course, they will generally be directed to those objects which are the most productive, and this in a more certain and direct manner than the wisdom of the most enlightened legislature could point out.

—James Madison, speech to the Congress, Apr. 9, 1789

May 16

One single object [will merit] the endless gratitude of the society: that of restraining the judges from usurping legislation. . . . They are practicing on the Constitution by inferences, analogies, and sophisms, as they would on an ordinary law. They do not seem aware that it is not even a Constitution formed by a single authority, and subject to a single superintendence and control; but that it is a compact of many independent powers, every single one of which claims an equal right to understand it, and to require its observance.

—Thomas Jefferson to Edward Livingston,
Mar. 25, 1825

May 17

Since private and public vices, are in reality, though not always apparently, so nearly connected, of how much importance, how necessary is it, that the utmost pains be taken by the public, to have the principles of virtue early inculcated on the minds even of children, and the moral sense kept alive, and that the wise institutions of our ancestors for these great purposes be encouraged by the government.

For no people will tamely surrender their liberties, nor can any be easily subdued, when knowledge is diffused and virtue is preserved. On the contrary, when people are universally ignorant, and debauched in their manners, they will sink under their own weight without the aid of foreign invaders.

—Samuel Adams to James Warren, Nov. 4, 1775

May 18

Security being the true design and end of government, it unanswerably follows that whatever form thereof appears most likely to ensure it to us, with the least expense and greatest benefit, is preferable to all others. . . . I draw my idea of the form of government from a principle in nature which no art can overturn, viz., that the more simple any thing is, the less liable it is to be disordered, and the easier repaired when disordered.

—Thomas Paine, *Common Sense,* 1776

May 19

The equal rights of man, and the happiness of every individual, are now acknowledged to be the only legitimate objects of government. Modern times have the signal advantage, too, of having discovered the only device by which these rights can be secured, to wit: government by the people, acting not in person, but by representatives chosen by themselves, that is to say; by every man of ripe years and sane mind, who either contributes by his purse or person to the support of his country.

—Thomas Jefferson to A. Coray, Oct. 31, 1823

May 20

Citizens, by birth or choice, of a common country, that country has a right to concentrate your affections. The name of American, which belongs to you in your national capacity, must always exalt the just pride of patriotism more than any appellation derived from local discriminations. With slight shades of difference, you have the same religion, manners, habits, and political principles. You have in a common cause fought and triumphed together; the independence and liberty you possess are the work of joint counsels, and joint efforts of common dangers, sufferings, and successes. . . . Every portion of our country finds the most commanding motives for carefully guarding and preserving the union of the whole.

—George Washington, Farewell Address, Sept. 19, 1796

May 21

A Constitution is, in fact, and must be regarded by the judges, as a fundamental law. It therefore belongs to them to ascertain its meaning, as well as the meaning of any particular act proceeding from the legislative body. If there should happen to be an irreconcilable variance between the two, . . . the Constitution ought to be preferred to the statute, the intention of the people to the intention of their agents.

Nor does this conclusion by any means suppose a superiority of the judicial to the legislative power. It only supposes that the power of the people is superior to both; and that where the will of the legislature, declared in its statutes, stands in opposition to that of the people, declared in the Constitution, the judges ought to be governed by the latter rather than the former. They ought to regulate their decisions by the fundamental laws, rather than by those which are not fundamental. . . .

Whenever a particular statute contravenes the Constitution, it will be the duty of the judicial tribunals to adhere to the latter and disregard the former.

—Alexander Hamilton, Federalist No. 78, 1788

May 22

The man who is possessed of wealth, who lolls on his sofa, or rolls in his carriage, cannot judge of the wants or feelings of the day laborer. The government we mean to erect is intended to last for ages. . . . unless wisely provided against, what will become of your government? In England, at this day, if elections were open to all classes of people, the property of the landed proprietors would be insecure. An agrarian law would soon take place. If these observations be just, our government ought to secure the permanent interests of the country against innovation. Landholders ought to have a share in the government, to support these invaluable interests, and to balance and check the other. They ought to be so constituted as to protect the minority of the opulent against the majority. The senate, therefore, ought to be this body; and to answer these purposes.

—James Madison, Constitutional Convention,
June 26, 1787

May 23

The liberties of our country, the freedom of our civil Constitution are worth defending at all hazards; and it is our duty to defend them against all attacks. We have received them as a fair inheritance from our worthy ancestors. They purchased them for us with toil, and danger, and expense of treasure and blood, and transmitted them to us with care and diligence. It will bring an everlasting mark of infamy on the present generation, enlightened as it is, if we should suffer them to be wrested from us by violence without a struggle, or be cheated out of them by the artifices of false and designing men. Of the latter, we are in most danger at present. Let us therefore be aware of it. Let us contemplate our forefathers and posterity, and resolve to maintain the rights bequeathed to us from the former for the sake of the latter.

—Samuel Adams, writing as Candidus,
Boston Gazette, Oct. 14, 1771

May 24

Although in the circle of his friends, where he might be unreserved with safety, he took a free share in conversation his colloquial talents were not above mediocrity, possessing neither copiousness of ideas, nor fluency of words. In public, when called on for a sudden opinion, he was unready, short and embarrassed.

—Thomas Jefferson to Dr. Walter Jones,
Jan. 2, 1814

May 25

I hope the great business of elections will never be left by the many, to be done by the few; for before we are aware of it, that few may become the engine of corruption. . . . Heaven forbid! that our countrymen should ever be biased in their choice, by unreasonable predilections for any man, or that an attachment to the Constitution . . . should be lost in devotion to persons. The effect of this would soon be, to change the love of liberty into the spirit of faction. Let each citizen remember, at the moment he is offering his vote, . . . that he is executing one of the most solemn trusts in human society, for which he is accountable to GOD and his country.

—Samuel Adams, in the *Boston Gazette,*
Apr. 16, 1781

May 26

If [Great Britain] is determined to enslave us, it must be by force of arms; and to attempt this, I again assert, would be nothing less than *the grossest infatuation, madness itself.*

Whatever may be said of the disciplined troops of Great Britain, the event of the contest must be extremely doubtful. There is a certain enthusiasm in liberty, that makes human nature rise above itself in acts of bravery and heroism. It cannot be expected that America would yield, without a magnanimous, persevering, and bloody struggle. The testimony of past ages, and the least knowledge of mankind, must suffice to convince us of the contrary . . . ; and if we take a view of the colonies in general, we must perceive that the pulse of Americans beats high in their country's cause.

> —Alexander Hamilton, "The Farmer Refuted,"
> Feb. 23, 1775

May 27

All, too, will bear in mind this sacred principle, that though the will of the majority is in all cases to prevail, that will to be rightful must be reasonable; that the minority possess their equal rights, which equal law must protect, and to violate would be oppression. Let us, then, fellow-citizens, unite with one heart and one mind. Let us restore to social intercourse that harmony and affection without which liberty and even life itself are but dreary things.

> —Thomas Jefferson, First Inaugural Address,
> Mar. 4, 1801

May 28

If the federal government should overpass the just
bounds of its authority and make a tyrannical use of
its powers, the people, whose creature it is, must appeal to the standard they have formed, and take such
measures to redress the injury done to the Constitution
as the exigency may suggest and prudence justify. The
propriety of a law, in a constitutional light, must always
be determined by the nature of the powers upon which
it is founded.

—Alexander Hamilton, Federalist No. 33, 1788

May 29

The powers delegated by the proposed Constitution to
the federal government are few and defined. Those
which are to remain in the state governments are numerous and indefinite. The former will be exercised prin-
cipally on external objects, as war, peace, negotiation
and foreign commerce. . . . The powers reserved to the
several states will extend to all the objects which in the
ordinary course of affairs, concern the lives and liberties,
and properties of the people, and the internal order,
improvement and prosperity of the state.

—James Madison, Federalist No. 45, 1788

May 30

In the supposed state of nature, all men are equally
bound by the laws of nature, or to speak more properly,
the laws of the Creator:—They are imprinted by the
finger of God on the heart of man. . . . In the state of

nature, every man hath an equal right by honest means to acquire property, and to enjoy it; in general, to pursue his own happiness, and none can consistently control or interrupt him in the pursuit. But, so turbulent are the passions of some, and so selfish the feelings of others, that in such a state, there being no social compact, the weak cannot always be protected from the violence of the strong, nor the honest and unsuspecting from the arts and intrigues of the selfish and cunning. Hence it is easy to conceive, that men, naturally formed for society, were inclined to enter into mutual compact for the better security of their natural rights. In this state of society, the unalienable rights of nature are held sacred.

—Samuel Adams to the Legislature of Massachusetts,
Jan. 17, 1794

May 31

It . . . astonishes me, Sir, to find this system approaching so near to perfection as it does; and I think it will astonish our enemies, who are waiting with confidence to hear that our councils are confounded like those of the builders of Babel; and that our states are on the point of separation, only to meet hereafter for the purpose of cutting one another's throats. Thus I consent, Sir, to this Constitution because I expect no better, and because I am not sure, that it is not the best.

—Benjamin Franklin, Constitutional Convention,
Sept. 17, 1787

JUNE

June 1

The praise of affording a just securing to property, should be sparingly bestowed on a government which, however scrupulously guarding the possessions of individuals, does not protect them in the enjoyment and communication of their opinions, in which they have an equal, and in the estimation of some, a more valuable property.

More sparingly should this praise be allowed to a government, where a man's religious rights are violated. . . . Conscience is the most sacred of all property.

—James Madison, essay on Property, Mar. 29, 1792

June 2

Cherish . . . the spirit of our people, and keep alive their attention. Do not be too severe upon their errors, but reclaim them by enlightening them. If once they become inattentive to the public affairs, you and I, and Congress, and assemblies, judges, and governors, shall all become wolves.

—Thomas Jefferson to Edward Carrington,
Jan. 16, 1787

June 3

There is a mystery in the countenance of some causes, which we have not always present judgment enough to explain. It is distressing to see an enemy advancing into a country, but it is the only place in which we can beat them, and in which we have always beaten them, whenever they made the attempt. The nearer any disease approaches to a crisis, the nearer it is to a cure. Danger and deliverance make their advances together, and it is only the last push, in which one or the other takes the lead.

—Thomas Paine, *American Crisis*, no. 4,
Sept. 11, 1776

June 4

It would be peculiarly improper to omit in this first official act, my fervent supplications to that Almighty Being who rules over the universe, who presides in the councils of nations, and whose providential aids can supply every human defect, that his benediction may consecrate to the liberties and happiness of the people of the United States, a government instituted by themselves for these essential purposes: and may enable every instrument employed in its administration to execute with success, the functions allotted to his charge. In tendering this homage to the Great Author of every public and private good, I assure myself that it expresses your sentiments not less than my own.

—George Washington, First Inaugural Address,
Apr. 30, 1789

June 5

It is of great importance to set a resolution, not to be shaken, never to tell an untruth. There is no vice so mean, so pitiful, so contemptible; and he who permits himself to tell a lie once, finds it much easier to do it a second and a third time, till at length it becomes habitual; he tells lies without attending to it, and truths without the world's believing him. This falsehood of the tongue leads to that of the heart, and in time depraves all its good disposition.

—Thomas Jefferson to his nephew Peter Carr,
Aug. 19, 1785

June 6

To the evil of monarchy we have added that of hereditary succession; and as the first is a degradation and lessening of ourselves, so the second, claimed as a matter of right, is an insult and imposition on posterity. For all men being originally equals, no one by birth could have the right to set up his own family in perpetual preference to all others forever, and though himself might deserve some decent degree of honors of his contemporaries, yet his descendants might be far too unworthy to inherit them.

—Thomas Paine, *Common Sense,* 1776

June 7

Government is instituted for the common good; for the protection, safety, prosperity, and happiness of the people; and not for profit, honor, or private interest of any one man, family, or class of men; therefore, the people

alone have an incontestable, unalienable, and indefeasible right to institute government; and to reform, alter,
or totally change the same, when their protection, safety,
prosperity, and happiness require it.

—John Adams, *Thoughts on Government*, 1776

June 8

As the people are the only legitimate fountain of power,
and it is from them that the constitutional charter, under
which the several branches of government hold their
power, is derived, it seems strictly consonant to the republican theory, to recur to the same original authority,
not only whenever it may be necessary to enlarge, dimin-
ish, or new-model the powers of the government, but
also whenever any one of the departments may commit
encroachments on the chartered authorities of the others.

—James Madison, Federalist No. 49, 1788

June 9

Until the people have, by some solemn and authoritative
act, annulled or changed the established form, it is bind-
ing upon themselves collectively, as well as individually;
and no presumption, or even knowledge of their sentiments, can warrant their representatives in a departure
from it, prior to such an act. But it is easy to see, that
it would require an uncommon portion of fortitude in
the judges to do their duty as faithful guardians of the
Constitution, where legislative invasions of it had been
instigated by the major voice of the community.

—Alexander Hamilton, Federalist No. 78, 1788

June 10

It is with great sincerity I join you in acknowledging and admiring the dispensations of Providence in our favor. America has only to be thankful and to persevere. God will finish his work, and establish their freedom. And the lovers of liberty will flock, from all parts of Europe with their fortunes to participate with us of that freedom, as soon as the peace is restored.

—Benjamin Franklin to Josiah Quincy, Apr. 22, 1779

June 11

Power always sincerely, conscientiously, *de très bon foi* [very candidly], believes itself right. Power always thinks it has a great soul and vast views, beyond the comprehension of the weak; and that it is doing God service, when it is violating all his laws. Our passions, ambition, avarice, love, resentment, etc., possess so much metaphysical subtlety and so much overpowering eloquence, that they insinuate themselves into the understanding and the conscience and convert both to their party. . . . I say that power must never be trusted without a check.

—John Adams to Thomas Jefferson, Feb. 2, 1816

June 12

There are virtues and vices which are properly called *political*. "Corruption, dishonesty to one's country, luxury, and extravagance tend to the ruin of states." The opposite virtues tend to their establishment. . . . Therefore, "wise and able politicians will guard against other vices," and be attentive to promote every virtue. He who is void of virtuous attachments in private life is, or very soon will be, void of all regard for his country. There is seldom an instance of a man guilty of betraying his country, who had not before lost the feeling of moral obligations in his private connections.

—Samuel Adams to James Warren, Nov. 4, 1775

June 13

Laws are made for men of ordinary understanding and should, therefore, be construed by the ordinary rules of common sense. Their meaning is not to be sought for in metaphysical subtleties which may make anything mean everything or nothing at pleasure. . . . The states supposed that by their tenth amendment, they had secured themselves against constructive powers.

—Thomas Jefferson to William Johnson,
June 12, 1823

June 14

Knowledge is, in every country, the surest basis of public happiness. . . . To the security of a free constitution it contributes in various ways: by convincing those who are entrusted with the public administration, that every valuable end of government is best answered by the enlightened confidence of the people; and by teaching the people themselves to know and to value their own rights; to discern and provide against invasions of them; to distinguish between oppression and the necessary exercise of lawful authority; between burthens proceeding from a disregard to their convenience, and those resulting from the inevitable exigencies of society; to discriminate the spirit of liberty from that of licentiousness—cherishing the first, avoiding the last; and uniting a speedy but temperate vigilance against encroachments, with an inviolable respect to the laws.

—George Washington, First Annual Message,
Jan. 8, 1790

June 15

When men enter into society, it is by voluntary consent; and they have a right to demand and insist upon the performance of such conditions and previous limitations as form an equitable original compact. Every natural right not expressly given up, or, from the nature of a social compact, necessarily ceded, remains. All positive and civil laws should conform, as far as possible, to the law of natural reason and equity.

—Samuel Adams, "The Rights of the Colonists," 1772

June 16

No government can continue good but under the control of the people; and . . . . their minds are to be informed by education what is right and what wrong; to be encouraged in habits of virtue and to be deterred from those of vice . . . ; in all cases, to follow truth as the only safe guide, and to eschew error, which bewilders us in one false consequence after another in endless succession. These are the inculcations necessary to render the people a sure basis for the structure and order of government.

—Thomas Jefferson to John Adams,
Dec. 10, 1819

June 17

I have lived, Sir, a long time, and the longer I live, the more convincing proofs I see of this truth—*That God governs the affairs of men.* And if a sparrow cannot fall to the ground without His notice, is it probable that an empire can rise without His aid?

We have been assured, sir, in the sacred writings, that "except the Lord build the house, they labor in vain that build it." I firmly believe this; and I also believe that without his concurring aid we shall succeed in this political building no better than the builders of Babel: We shall be divided by our partial local interests; our projects will be confounded, and we ourselves shall become a reproach and bye word down to future ages. And what is worse, mankind may hereafter from this unfortunate instance, despair of establishing governments by human wisdom and leave it to chance, war and conquest.

—Benjamin Franklin, Constitutional Convention,
June 28, 1787

June 18

Our country is too large to have all its affairs directed by a single government. Public servants at such a distance, and from under the eye of their constituents, must, from the circumstance of distance, be unable to administer and overlook all the details necessary for the good government of the citizens; and the same circumstance, by rendering detection impossible to their constituents, will invite public agents to corruption, plunder and waste.

—Thomas Jefferson to Gideon Granger,
Aug. 13, 1800

June 19

Since the general civilization of mankind, I believe there are more instances of the abridgment of the freedom of the people by gradual and silent encroachments of those in power, than by violent and sudden usurpations; but, on a candid examination of history, we shall find that turbulence, violence, and abuse of power, by the majority trampling on the rights of the minority, have produced factions and commotions, which, in republics, have, more frequently than any other cause, produced despotism. If we go over the whole history of ancient and modern republics, we shall find their destruction to have generally resulted from those causes.

—James Madison, Virginia Ratifying Convention,
June 6, 1788

June 20

Our cause is just. Our union is perfect. . . . We gratefully acknowledge . . . that his Providence would not permit us to be called into this severe controversy, until we were grown up to our present strength. . . . With hearts fortified with these animating reflections, we most solemnly, before God and the world, declare, that, exerting the utmost energy of those powers, which our beneficent Creator hath graciously bestowed upon us, the arms we have compelled by our enemies to assume, we will, in defiance of every hazard, with unabating firmness and perseverance employ for the preservation of our liberties; being with one mind resolved to die freemen rather than to live as slaves.

—Thomas Jefferson, "Declaration of the Causes and
Necessity of Taking up Arms," July 6, 1775

June 21

I, sir, have always conceived—I believe those who proposed the Constitution conceived—it is still more fully
known, and more material to observe, that those who
ratified the Constitution conceived—that this is not an
indefinite government, deriving its powers from the general terms prefixed to the specified powers—but a limited
government, tied down to the specified powers, which
explain and define the general terms.

—James Madison, congressional debate
on the cod fishery bill, Feb. 7, 1792

June 22

If a nation expects to be ignorant and free, in a state of
civilization, it expects what never was and never will be.
The functionaries of every government have propensities
to command at will the liberty and property of their
constituents. There is no safe deposit for these but with
the people themselves; nor can they be safe with them
without information. Where the press is free, and every
man able to read, all is safe.

—Thomas Jefferson to Colonel Charles Yancey,
Jan. 6, 1816

June 23

A general dissolution of the principles and manners will
more surely overthrow the liberties of America than the
whole force of the common enemy. . . . While the people are virtuous they cannot be subdued; but once they
lose their virtue, they will be ready to surrender their

liberties to the first external or internal invader. How necessary then is it for those who are determined to transmit the blessings of liberty as a fair inheritance to posterity, to associate on public principles in support of public virtue. If virtue and knowledge are diffused among the people, they will never be enslaved. This will be their great security.

—Samuel Adams to James Warren, Feb. 12, 1779

June 24

The example of changing a constitution by assembling the wise men of the state, instead of assembling armies, will be worth as much to the world as the former examples we had given them. The constitution, too, which was the result of our deliberation, is unquestionably the wisest ever yet presented to men.

—Thomas Jefferson to David Humphreys, Mar. 18, 1789

June 25

The federal and state governments are in fact but different agents and trustees of the people, constituted with different powers, and designed for different purposes. The adversaries of the Constitution seem to have lost sight of the people altogether in their reasonings on this subject; and to have viewed these different establishments, not only as mutual rivals and enemies, but as uncontrolled by any common superior in their efforts to usurp the authorities of each other. [But] . . . the ultimate authority, wherever the derivative may be found, resides in the people alone, and . . . it will not depend merely on the comparative ambition or address of the different governments, whether either, or which of them, will be able to enlarge its sphere of jurisdiction at the expense of the other. Truth, no less than decency, requires that the event in every case should be supposed to depend on the sentiments and sanction of their common constituents.

—James Madison, Federalist 46, 1788

June 26

I really look with commiseration over the great body of my fellow citizens, who, reading newspapers, live and die in the belief, that they have known something of what has been passing in the world in their time. . . .The man who never looks into a newspaper is better informed than he who reads them, inasmuch as he who knows nothing is nearer to truth than he whose mind is filled with falsehoods and errors.

—Thomas Jefferson to John Norvell, June 14, 1807

June 27

The eyes of mankind will be upon you to see whether the government, which is now more popular than it has been for many years past, will be productive of more virtue, moral and political. We may look up to armies for our defense, but virtue is our best security. It is not possible that any state should long remain free, where virtue is not supremely honored.

—Samuel Adams to James Warren, Nov. 4, 1775

June 28

A fondness for power is implanted in most men, and it is natural to abuse it when acquired. This maxim, drawn from the experience of all ages, makes it the height of folly to entrust any set of men with power which is not under every possible control; perpetual strides are made after more as long as there is any part withheld. We ought not, therefore, to concede any greater authority to the [government] than is absolutely necessary.

—Alexander Hamilton, "The Farmer Refuted,"
Feb. 23, 1775

June 29

The members of the legislative department . . . are numerous. They are distributed and dwell among the people at large. Their connections of blood, of friendship, and of acquaintance embrace a great proportion of the most influential part of the society . . . they are more immediately the confidential guardians of their rights and liberties.

—James Madison, Federalist No. 50, 1788

June 30

Property is surely a right of mankind as really as liberty. Perhaps, at first, prejudice, habit, shame or fear, principle or religion, would restrain the poor from attacking the rich, and the idle from usurping on the industrious; but the time would not be long before courage and enterprise would come, and pretexts be invented by degrees, to countenance the majority in dividing all the property among them, or at least, in sharing it equally with its present possessors. Debts would be abolished first; taxes laid heavy on the rich, and not at all on the others; and at last a downright equal division of everything be demanded, and voted. . . . The moment the idea is admitted into society that property is not as sacred as the laws of God, and that there is not a force of law and public justice to protect it, anarchy and tyranny commence. If "Thou shalt not covet" and "Thou shalt not steal" were not commandments of Heaven, they must be made inviolable precepts in every society before it can be civilized or made free.

—John Adams, *A Defense of the Constitutions of Government of the United States of America,* 1787

JULY

July 1

Be it remembered . . . that liberty must at all hazards
be supported. We have a right to it, derived from our
Maker. But if we have not, our fathers have earned and
bought it for us at the expense of their ease, their estates,
their pleasure, and their blood. And liberty cannot be
preserved without a general knowledge among the people, who have a right, from the frame of their nature,
to knowledge, as their great Creator, who does nothing
in vain, has given them understandings, and a desire
to know.

—John Adams, *A Dissertation on the
Canon and Feudal Law*, 1765

July 2

The second day of July, 1776, will be the most memo-
rable epoch in the history of America. I am apt to believe
that it will be celebrated by succeeding generations as the
great anniversary festival. It ought to be commemorated,
as the day of deliverance, by solemn acts of devotion to
God Almighty. It ought to be solemnized with pomp and
parade, with shows, games, sports, guns, bells, bonfires

and illuminations, from one end of this continent to the other, from this time forward forever. You will think me transported with enthusiasm, but I am not.

—John Adams to Abigail Adams, July 3, 1776
(July 4 actually became known as Independence Day because that was the day the actual Declaration was formally approved.)

July 3

It always has been, and will continue to be, my earnest desire to learn, and to comply, as far as is consistent, with the public sentiment; but it is on great occasions only, and after time has been given for cool and deliberate reflection, that the real voice of the people can be known.

—George Washington to Edward Carrington,
May 1, 1796

July 4

We hold these truths to be self-evident, that all men are created equal; that they are endowed by their Creator with inherent and inalienable rights; that among these, are life, liberty, and the pursuit of happiness; that to secure these rights, governments are instituted among men, deriving their just powers from the consent of the governed; that whenever any form of government becomes destructive of these ends, it is the right of the people to alter or abolish it, and to institute new government, laying its foundation on such principles, and organizing its powers in such form, as to them shall seem most likely to effect their safety and happiness.

—Thomas Jefferson, Declaration
of Independence, 1776

July 5

We are either a united people, or we are not. If the former, let us, in all matters of general concern act as a nation, which have national objects to promote, and a national character to support. If we are not, let us no longer act a farce by pretending to it.

—George Washington to James Madison,
Nov. 30, 1785

July 6

The proposed Constitution, so far from implying an abolition of the state governments, makes them constituent parts of the national sovereignty, by allowing them a direct representation in the Senate, and leaves in their possession certain exclusive and very important portions of sovereign power. This fully corresponds, in every rational import of the terms, with the idea of a federal government.

—Alexander Hamilton, Federalist No. 9, 1787
(Unfortunately, this aspect of the Constitution
was nullified by the 17th amendment.)

July 7

We may appeal to every page of history we have hitherto turned over, for proofs irrefragable, that the people, when they have been unchecked, have been as unjust, tyrannical, brutal, barbarous and cruel as any king or senate possessed of uncontrollable power. . . .

All projects of government, formed upon a supposition of continual vigilance, sagacity, and virtue, firmness of the people, when possessed of the exercise of supreme power, are cheats and delusions. The people are the fountain of power; they must, in their constitution, appoint different orders to watch one another, and give them the alarm in time of danger. . . . Then, and then only, can the people hope to be warned of every danger, and be put constantly on their guard, kept constantly vigilant, penetrating, virtuous, and steady.

—John Adams, *A Defence of the Constitutions of Government*, 1787

July 8

There is a natural aristocracy among men. The grounds of this are virtue and talents. . . . The natural aristocracy I consider as the most precious gift of nature for the instruction, the trusts, and government of society. And indeed it would have been inconsistent in creation to have formed man for the social state, and not to have provided virtue and wisdom enough to manage the concerns of the society.

—Thomas Jefferson to John Adams, Oct. 28, 1813

July 9

It is substantially true, that virtue or morality is a necessary spring of popular government. The rule indeed extends with more or less force to every species of free government. Who that is a sincere friend to it, can look with indifference upon attempts to shake the foundation of the fabric?

—George Washington, Farewell Address, Sept. 19, 1796

July 10

Ambition must be made to counteract ambition. The interest of the man must be connected with the constitutional rights of the place. It may be a reflection on human nature that such devices should be necessary to control the abuses of government. But what is government itself, but the greatest of all reflections on human nature? If men were angels, no government would be necessary. If angels were to govern men, neither external nor internal controls on government would be necessary.

—James Madison, Federalist No. 51, 1788

July 11

If virtue and knowledge are diffused among the people, they will never be enslaved. This will be their great security. Virtue and knowledge will forever be an even balance for powers and riches. I hope our countrymen will never depart from the principles and maxims which have been handed down to us from our wise forefathers. This greatly depends upon the example of men of character and influence of the present day.

—Samuel Adams to James Warren,
Feb. 12, 1779

July 12

At the establishment of our constitutions, the judiciary bodies were supposed to be the most helpless and harmless members of the government. Experience, however, soon showed in what way they were to become the most dangerous; that the insufficiency of the means provided for their removal gave them a freehold and irresponsibility in office; that their decisions, seeming to concern individual suitors only, pass silent and unheeded by the public at large; that these decisions, nevertheless, become law by precedent, sapping, by little and little, the foundations of the constitution, and working its change by construction, before any one has perceived that that invisible and helpless worm has been busily employed in consuming its substance. In truth, man is not made to be trusted for life, if secured against all liability to account.

—Thomas Jefferson to A. Coray, Oct. 31, 1823

July 13

To argue with a man who has renounced the use and authority of reason, and whose philosophy consists in holding humanity in contempt, is like administering medicine to the dead, or endeavoring to convert an atheist by scripture. Enjoy, sir, your insensibility of feeling and reflecting. It is the prerogative of animals. And no man will envy you these honors, in which a savage only can be your rival and a bear your master.

—Thomas Paine, *American Crisis,* no. 5,
Mar. 21, 1777

July 14

When occasions present themselves in which the interests of the people are at variance with their inclinations, it is the duty of the persons whom they have appointed to be the guardians of those interests to withstand the temporary delusion in order to give them time and opportunity for more cool and sedate reflection. Instances might be cited in which a conduct of this kind has saved the people from very fatal consequences of their own mistakes, and has procured lasting monuments of their gratitude to the men who had courage and magnanimity enough to serve them at the peril of their displeasure.

—Alexander Hamilton, Federalist No. 71, 1788

July 15

Convinced that the republican is the only form of government which is not eternally at open or secret war with the rights of mankind, my prayers and efforts shall be cordially distributed to the support of that we have so happily established. It is an animating thought that, while we are securing the rights of ourselves and our posterity, we are pointing out the way to struggling nations who wish, like us, to emerge from their tyrannies also. Heaven help their struggles, and lead them, as it has done us, triumphantly thro' them.

—Thomas Jefferson to William Hunter,
Mar. 11, 1790

July 16

It matters not where you live, or what rank of life you hold, the evil or the blessing [of the war] will reach you all. The far and the near, the home counties and the back, the rich and the poor, will suffer or rejoice alike. The heart that feels not now is dead; the blood of his children will curse his cowardice, who shrinks back at a time when a little might have saved the whole, and made them happy. I love the man that can smile in trouble, that can gather strength from distress, and grow brave by reflection. 'Tis the business of little minds to shrink; but he whose heart is firm, and whose conscience approves his conduct, will pursue his principles unto death.

—Thomas Paine, *American Crisis,* no. 1,
Dec. 23, 1776

July 17

Have you ever found in history, one single example of a nation thoroughly corrupted that was afterwards restored to virtue? And without virtue, there can be no political liberty. . . . Will you tell me how to prevent riches from becoming the effects of temperance and industry? Will you tell me how to prevent luxury from producing effeminacy, intoxication, extravagance, vice, and folly? . . . I believe no effort in favor of virtue is lost.

—John Adams to Thomas Jefferson, Dec. 18, 1819

July 18

Government is instituted to protect property of every sort; as well that which lies in the various rights of individuals, as that which the term particularly expresses. This being the end of government, that alone is a *just* government which *impartially* secures to every man whatever is his *own.* . . .

That is not a just government, nor is property secure under it, where the property which a man has in his personal safety and personal liberty, is violated by arbitrary seizures of one class of citizens for the service of the rest.

— James Madison, "Essay on Property," 1792

July 19

Let divines, and philosophers, statesmen and patriots unite their endeavors to renovate the age, by impressing the minds of men with the importance of educating their little boys, and girls—of inculcating in the minds of youth the fear, and love of the Deity, and universal philanthropy; and in subordination to these great principles, the love of their country—of instructing them in the art of self-government, without which they never can act a wise part in the government of societies great, or small—in short of leading them in the study, and practice of the exalted virtues of the Christian system.

—Samuel Adams to John Adams, Oct. 4, 1790

July 20

Leave no authority existing not responsible to the people; whose rights, however, to the exercise of fruits of their own industry, can never be protected against the selfishness of rulers not subject to their control at short periods. . . . My most earnest wish is to see the republican element of popular control pushed to the maximum of its practicable exercise. I shall then believe that our government may be pure and perpetual.

—Thomas Jefferson to Isaac H. Tiffany, Aug. 26, 1816

July 21

Happily for America, happily, we trust, for the whole human race, they pursued a new and more noble course. They accomplished a revolution which has no parallel in the annals of human society. They reared the fabrics of governments which have no model on the face of the globe. They formed the design of a great confederacy, which it is incumbent on their successors to improve and perpetuate.

—James Madison, Federalist No. 14, 1787

July 22

I cannot contemplate human affairs, without laughing or crying. I choose to laugh. When people talk of the freedom of writing, speaking, or thinking, I cannot choose but laugh. No such thing ever existed. No such thing now exists; but I hope it will exist. But it must be hundreds of years after you and I shall write and speak no more.

—John Adams to Thomas Jefferson, July 15, 1817

July 23

I have long been convinced that our enemies have made it an object, to eradicate from the minds of the people in general a sense of true religion and virtue, in hopes thereby the more easily to carry their point of enslaving them. . . . Revelation assures us that "righteousness exalteth a nation."—Communities are dealt with in this world by the wise and just ruler of the universe. He rewards or punishes them according to their general character. The diminution of public virtue is usually attended with that of public happiness, and the public liberty will not long survive the total extinction of morals. . . . Could I be assured that America would remain virtuous, I would venture to defy the utmost efforts of enemies to subjugate her. You will allow me to remind you, that the morals of that city which has born so great a share in the American contest, depend much upon the vigilance of the respectable body of magistrates of which you are a member.

—Samuel Adams to John Scollay, Apr. 30, 1776

July 24

With respect to our state and federal governments, I do not think their relations correctly understood by foreigners. They generally suppose the former subordinate to the latter. But this is not the case. They are coordinate departments of one simple and integral whole. To the state governments are reserved all legislation and administration, in affairs which concern their own citizens only, and to the federal government is given whatever concerns foreigners, or the citizens of other states; these functions alone being made federal. The one is the domestic, the other the foreign branch of the same government; neither having control over the other, but within its own department. There are one or two exceptions only to this partition of power.

—Thomas Jefferson to John Cartwright, June 5, 1824

July 25

I regret that I am now to die in the belief, that the useless sacrifice of themselves by the generation of 1776, to acquire self- government and happiness to their country, is to be thrown away by the unwise and unworthy passions of their sons, and that my only consolation is to be, that I live not to weep over it. If they would but dispassionately weigh the blessings they will throw away, against an abstract principle more likely to be effected by union than by scission, they would pause before they would perpetrate this act of suicide on themselves, and of treason against the hopes of the world. To yourself, as the faithful advocate of the Union, I tender the offering of my high esteem and respect.

—Thomas Jefferson to John Holmes, Apr. 22, 1820

July 26

The act . . . establishing the Constitution, will not be a *national*, but a *federal* act. . . . It is to result neither from the decision of a *majority* of the people of the union, nor from that of a *majority* of the states. It must result from the *unanimous* assent of the several states that are parties to it. . . . Each state, in ratifying the Constitution, is considered as a sovereign body, independent of all others, and only to be bound by its own voluntary act. In this relation, then, the new Constitution will, if established, be a *federal*, and not a *national* constitution.

—James Madison, Federalist No. 39, 1788

July 27

Our government is now taking so steady a course as to show by what road it will pass to destruction, to wit: by consolidation of power first, and then corruption, its necessary consequence. The engine of consolidation will be the federal judiciary; the other two branches the corrupting and corrupted instruments.

—Thomas Jefferson to Nathaniel Macon,
Nov. 23, 1821

July 28

If a number of political societies enter into a larger political society, the laws which the latter may enact, pursuant to the powers entrusted to it by its constitution, must necessarily be supreme over those societies and the individuals of whom they are composed. . . . But it will not follow from this doctrine that acts of the larger society which are *not pursuant* to its constitutional powers, but which are invasions of the residuary authorities of the smaller societies, will become the supreme law of the land. These will be merely acts of usurpation, and will deserve to be treated as such.

—Alexander Hamilton, Federalist No. 33, 1788

July 29

The eyes of the people are upon us. . . . If we despond, . . . the people will no longer yield their support to a hopeless contest, and American liberty is no more. . . . Despondency becomes not the dignity of our cause, nor the character of those who are its supporters. Let us awaken then, and evince a different spirit—a spirit that shall inspire the people with confidence in themselves and in us—a spirit that will encourage them to persevere in this glorious struggle, until their rights and liberties shall be established on a rock. We have proclaimed to the world our determination "to die freemen, rather than to live slaves." We have appealed to Heaven for the justice of our cause, and in Heaven we have placed our trust. . . . We shall never be abandoned by Heaven while we act worthy of its aid and protection.

—Samuel Adams, speech to Continental Congress, Sept. 1777

July 30

Statesmen, my dear sir, may plan and speculate for liberty, but it is religion and morality alone, which can establish the principles upon which freedom can securely stand. The only foundation of a free constitution is pure virtue, and if this cannot be inspired into our people in a greater measure than they have it now, they may change their rulers and the forms of government, but they will not obtain a lasting liberty. They will only exchange tyrants and tyrannies.

—John Adams to Zabdiel Adams, June 21, 1776

July 31

A just security to property is not afforded by that government, under which unequal taxes oppress one species of property and reward another species: where arbitrary taxes invade the domestic sanctuaries of the rich, and excessive taxes grind the faces of the poor; where the keenness and competitions of want are deemed an insufficient spur to labor, and taxes are again applied, by an unfeeling policy, as another spur; in violation of that sacred property, which Heaven, in decreeing man to earn his bread by the sweat of his brow, kindly reserved to him, in the small repose that could be spared from the supply of his necessities.

—James Madison, "Essay on Property," Mar. 1792

AUGUST

August 1

A good moral character is the first essential in a man, and that the habits contracted at your age are generally indelible, and your conduct here may stamp your character through life. It is therefore highly important that you should endeavor not only to be learned but virtuous.

—George Washington to Steptoe Washington,
Dec. 5, 1790

August 2

The most fortunate of us, in our journey through life, frequently meet with calamities and misfortunes which may greatly afflict us; and, to fortify our minds against the attacks of these calamities and misfortunes, should be one of the principal studies and endeavors of our lives. The only method of doing this is to assume a perfect resignation to the Divine will, to consider that whatever does happen, must happen; and that by our uneasiness, we cannot prevent the blow before it does fall, but we may add to its force after it has fallen. These considerations, and others such as these, may enable us in some measure to surmount the difficulties thrown in our way; to bear up with a tolerable degree of patience under this burthen of life; and to proceed with a pious and unshaken resignation, till we arrive at our journey's end, when we may deliver up our trust into the hands of him who gave it, and receive such reward as to him shall seem proportioned to our merit.

—Thomas Jefferson to John Page, July 15, 1763

August 3

The same conduct that best constitutes the safety of an individual, namely, a strict adherence to principle, constitutes also the safety of a government, and that without it safety is but an empty name. When the rich plunder the poor of his rights, it becomes an example of the poor to plunder the rich of his property, for the rights of the one are as much property to him as wealth is property to the other and the *little all* is as dear as the *much*. It is only by setting out on just principles that men are trained to be just to each other; and it will always be found, that when the rich protect the rights of the poor, the poor will protect the property of the rich.

—Thomas Paine, "Letter Addressed to the Addressers," 1792

August 4

The poor people, it is true, have been much less success-ful than the great. They have seldom found either leisure or opportunity to form a union and exert their strength; ignorant as they were of arts and letters, they have sel-dom been able to frame and support a regular opposition. This, however, has been known by the great to be the temper of mankind; and they have accordingly labored, in all ages, to wrest from the populace, as they are contemptuously called, the knowledge of their rights and wrongs, and the power to assert the former or redress the latter. I say RIGHTS, for such they have, undoubtedly, antecedent to all earthly government—Rights, that cannot be repealed or restrained by human laws—Rights, derived from the great Legislator of the universe.

—John Adams, *A Dissertation on the Canon and Feudal Law*, 1765

August 5

An elective despotism was not the government we fought for; but one in which the powers of government should be so divided and balanced among the several bodies of magistracy as that no one could transcend their legal limits without being effectually checked and restrained by the others.

—James Madison, Federalist No. 58, 1788

August 6

If, from the more wretched parts of the old world, we look at those which are in an advanced stage of improvement, we still find the greedy hand of government thrusting itself into every corner and crevice of industry, and grasping the spoil of the multitude. Invention is continually exercised, to furnish new pretenses for revenues and taxation. It watches prosperity as its prey and permits none to escape without tribute.

—Thomas Paine, *Rights of Man*, 1791

August 7

The moral sense, or conscience, is as much a part of man as his leg or arm. It is given to all human beings in a stronger or weaker degree, as force of members is given them in a greater or less degree. It may be strengthened by exercise, as may any particular limb of the body. This sense is submitted, indeed, in some degree, to the guidance of reason; but it is a small stock which is required for this: even a less one than what we call common sense. State a moral case to a ploughman and a professor. The former will decide it as well, and often better than the latter, because he has not been led astray by artificial rules.

—Thomas Jefferson to his nephew Peter Carr,
Aug. 10, 1787

August 8

Among the numerous advantages promised by a well-constructed Union, none deserves to be more accurately developed than its tendency to break and control the violence of faction.

—James Madison, Federalist No. 10, 1787

August 9

There is no part of the administration of government that requires extensive information and a thorough knowledge of the principles of political economy, so much as the business of taxation. The man who understands those principles best will be least likely to resort to oppressive expedients, or sacrifice any particular class of citizens to the procurement of revenue. It might be demonstrated that the most productive system of finance will always be the least burdensome.

—Alexander Hamilton, Federalist No. 35, 1788

August 10

Besides the advantage of being armed, which the Americans possess over the people of almost every other nation, the existence of subordinate governments, to which the people are attached, and by which the militia officers are appointed, forms a barrier against the enterprises of ambition, more insurmountable than any which a simple government of any form can admit of. Notwithstanding the military establishments in the several kingdoms of Europe, which are carried as far as the public resources will bear, the governments are afraid to trust the people with arms.

—James Madison, Federalist No. 46, 1788

August 11

The republican principle demands that the deliberate sense of the community should govern the conduct of those to whom they entrust the management of their affairs; but it does not require an unqualified complaisance to every sudden breeze of passion or to every transient impulse which the people may receive from the arts of men, who flatter their prejudices to betray their interests . . . , by the wiles of parasites and sycophants, by the snares of the ambitious, the avaricious, the desperate.

—Alexander Hamilton, Federalist No. 71, 1788

August 12

The object is great which we have in view, and we must expect a great expense of blood to obtain it. But we should always remember that a free constitution of civil government cannot be purchased at too dear a rate as there is nothing, on this side [of] the New Jerusalem, of equal importance to mankind.

—John Adams to Archibald Bullock, July 1, 1776

August 13

It behooves you, therefore, to think and act for yourself and your people. The great principles of right and wrong are legible to every reader; to pursue them requires not the aid of many counselors. The whole art of government consists in the art of being honest. Only aim to do your duty, and mankind will give you credit where you fail.

—Thomas Jefferson, *A Summary View of the Rights of British America*, July 1774

August 14

There is a rank due to the United States, among nations, which will be withheld, if not absolutely lost, by the reputation of weakness. If we desire to avoid insult, we must be able to repel it; if we desire to secure peace, one of the most powerful instruments of our rising prosperity, it must be known that we are at all times ready for war.

—George Washington, Fifth Annual Message to Congress, Dec. 3, 1793

August 15

In a free government, the security for civil rights must be the same as that for religious rights. It consists in the one case in the multiplicity of interests, and in the other in the multiplicity of sects. The degree of security in both cases, will depend on the number of interests and sects; and this may be presumed to depend on the extent of country and number of people comprehended under the same government.

—James Madison, Federalist No. 51, 1788

August 16

We are firmly convinced, and we act on that conviction, that with nations as with individuals our interests soundly calculated will ever be found inseparable from our moral duties, and history bears witness to the fact that a just nation is trusted on its word when recourse is had to armaments and wars to bridle others.

—Thomas Jefferson, Second Inaugural Address, Mar. 4, 1805

August 17

We cannot make events. Our business is wisely to improve them. There has been much to do to confirm doubting friends and fortify the timid. It requires time to bring honest men to think and determine alike even in important matters. Mankind are governed more by their feelings than by reason.

—Samuel Adams to Samuel Cooper, Apr. 30, 1776

August 18

Courage, then, my countrymen, our contest is not only whether we ourselves shall be free, but whether there shall be left to mankind an asylum on earth for civil and religious liberty. . . .

The hand of Heaven appears to have led us on to be, perhaps, humble instruments and means in the great providential dispensation which is completing. We have fled from the political Sodom; let us not look back lest we perish and become a monument of infamy and derision to the world. . . . The same force and resistance which are sufficient to procure us our liberties will secure us a glorious independence and support us in the dignity of free imperial states.

—Samuel Adams, speech, Pennsylvania State House,
Philadelphia, Aug. 1, 1776

August 19

When one side only of a story is heard and often repeated, the human mind becomes impressed with it insensibly.

—George Washington to Edmund Pendleton,
Jan. 22, 1795

August 20

It may be the will of Heaven that America shall suffer calamities still more wasting, and distresses yet more dreadful. If this is to be the case, it will have the good effect at least. It will inspire us with many virtues, which we have not, and correct many errors, follies and vices which threaten to disturb, dishonor, and destroy us. The furnace of affliction produces refinement, in states as well as individuals. And the new governments we are assuming in every part will require a purification from our vices, and an augmentation of our virtues, or they will be no blessings. The people will have unbounded power, and the people are extremely addicted to corruption and venality, as well as the great. But I must submit all my hopes and fears to an overruling Providence, in which, unfashionable as the faith may be, I firmly believe.

—John Adams to Abigail Adams, July 3, 1776

August 21

We sometimes meet with genuine republican sentiments in persons born under monarchy. It is truly mortifying when one meets with the reverse character. I firmly believe that the benevolent Creator designed the republican form of government for man. Will you venture so far as to say that all other institutions that we know of are unnatural and tend more or less to distress human societies?

—Samuel Adams to Richard Henry Lee,
Apr. 14, 1785

August 22

I cannot undertake to lay my finger on that article of the federal Constitution which granted a right to Congress of expending, on objects of benevolence, the money of their constituents.

—James Madison, speech in Congress, Jan. 10, 1794
(The expense in question was for French refugees
from the Haitian Revolution.)

August 23

Here is my creed: I believe in one God, the Creator of
the universe. That he governs it by his providence. That
he ought to be worshipped. That the most acceptable
service we render to him is in doing good to his other
children. That the soul of man is immortal, and will be
treated with justice in another life respecting its conduct
in this. These I take to be the fundamental points in all
sound religion.

—Benjamin Franklin to Ezra Stiles, Mar. 9, 1790

August 24

It is sufficiently obvious, that persons and property are
the two great subjects on which governments are to
act; and that the rights of persons, and the rights of
property, are the objects, for the protection of which
government was instituted. These rights cannot well be
separated. The personal right to acquire property, which
is a natural right, gives to property, when acquired, a
right to protection, as a social right.

—James Madison, Virginia Ratifying Convention,
Dec. 2, 1829

August 25

No people can be bound to acknowledge and adore the
invisible hand, which conducts the affairs of men more
than the people of the United States. Every step, by which
they have advanced to the character of an independent
nation, seems to have been distinguished by some token
of providential agency. And in the important revolution

just accomplished in the system of their united government, the tranquil deliberations and voluntary consent
of so many distinct communities, from which the event
has resulted, cannot be compared with the means by
which most governments have been established, without
some return of pious gratitude along with an humble
anticipation of the future blessings which the past seem
to presage.

—George Washington, First Inaugural Address,
Apr. 30, 1789

August 26

Let me . . . warn you in the most solemn manner against
the baneful effects of the spirit of party generally. . . .
It is a spirit not to be encouraged. . . . A fire not to be
quenched, it demands a uniform vigilance to prevent its
bursting into a flame, lest, instead of warming, it should
consume.

—George Washington, Farewell Address,
Sept. 19, 1796

August 27

History affords us many instances of the ruin of states,
by the prosecution of measures ill suited to the temper
and genius of their people. The ordaining of laws in
favor of one part of the nation, to the prejudice and
oppression of another, is certainly the most erroneous
and mistaken policy. An equal dispensation of protection,
rights, privileges, and advantages, is what every part is
entitled to, and ought to enjoy. . . . These measures never
fail to create great and violent jealousies and animosities

between the people favored and the people oppressed; whence a total separation of affections, interests, political obligations, and all manner of connections, by which the whole state is weakened.

—Benjamin Franklin, "Emblematical Representations," circa 1774

August 28

With respect to the words "general welfare," I have always regarded them as qualified by the detail of powers connected with them. To take them in a literal and unlimited sense would be a metamorphosis of the Constitution into a character which there is a host of proofs was not contemplated by its creators. If the words obtained so readily a place in the "Articles of Confederation," and received so little notice in their admission into the present Constitution, and retained for so long a time a silent place in both, the fairest explanation is, that the words in the alternative of meaning nothing or meaning everything, had the former meaning taken for granted.

—James Madison to James Robertson, Apr. 20, 1831

August 29

You be firm, my friends, nor let unmanly sloth twine round your hearts indissoluble chains; ne'er yet by force was freedom overcome, unless corruption first dejects the pride and guardian vigor of the free born soul; all crude attempts of violence are vain. Determined hold your independence; for, that once destroyed, unfounded freedom is a morning dream.

Let us remember that if we suffer tamely a lawless

attack upon our liberty, we encourage it, and involve others in our doom! It is a very serious consideration, which should deeply impress our minds, that millions yet unborn may be the miserable sharers in the event!

—Samuel Adams, writing as Candidus,
Boston Gazette, Oct. 14, 1771

August 30

A loan . . . threatens to saddle us with a perpetual debt. I hope a tax will be preferred, because it will awaken the attention of the people and make reformation and economy the principle of the next election. The frequent recurrence of this chastening operation can alone restrain the propensity of governments to enlarge expense beyond income.

—Thomas Jefferson to Albert Gallatin, Dec. 26, 1820

August 31

Our great security lies, I think, in our growing strength both in wealth and numbers, that creates an increasing ability of assisting this nation in its wars, which will make us more respectable, our friendship more valued, and our enmity feared; thence it will soon be thought proper to treat us, not with justice only, but with kindness; . . . unless by a neglect of military discipline we should lose all our martial spirit. . . . For there is much truth in the Italian saying, *Make yourselves sheep and the wolves will eat you.*

—Benjamin Franklin to Thomas Cushing,
Jan. 5, 1773

SEPTEMBER

September 1

The consequences of disunion cannot be too highly colored, or too often exhibited. Every man who loves peace, every man who loves his country, every man who loves liberty ought to have it ever before his eyes that he may cherish in his heart a due attachment to the union of America and be able to set a due value on the means of preserving it.

—James Madison, Federalist No. 41, 1788

September 2

I say, the earth belongs to each of these generations during its course, fully and in its own right. The second generation receives it clear of the debts and encumbrances of the first, the third of the second, and so on. For if the first could charge it with a debt, then the earth would belong to the dead and not to the living generation. Then, no generation can contract debts greater than may be paid during the course of its own existence.

—Thomas Jefferson to James Madison, Sept. 6, 1789

September 3

The belief in a God all-powerful, wise, and good, is so essential to the moral order of the world and to the happiness of man, that arguments which enforce it cannot be drawn from too many sources nor adapted with too much solicitude to the different characters and capacities to be impressed with it.

—James Madison to Rev. Frederick Beasley,
Nov. 20, 1825

September 4

The basis of our political systems is the right of the people to make and to alter their constitutions of government. But the constitution which at any time exists, till changed by an explicit and authentic act of the whole people, is sacredly obligatory upon all. The very idea of the power and the right of the people to establish government presupposes the duty of every individual to obey the established government.

—George Washington, Farewell Address,
Sept. 19, 1796

September 5

The existence of such a government as ours for any length of time is a full proof of a general dissemination of knowledge and virtue throughout the whole body of the people. And what object or consideration more pleasing than this can be presented to the human mind? If national pride is ever justifiable or excusable it is when it springs, not from power or riches, grandeur or glory, but from conviction of national innocence, information, and benevolence.

In the midst of these pleasing ideas we should be unfaithful to ourselves if we should ever lose sight of the danger to our liberties if anything partial or extraneous should infect the purity of our free, fair, virtuous, and independent elections.

—John Adams, Inaugural Address, Mar. 4, 1797

September 6

If circumstances should at any time oblige the government to form an army of any magnitude that army can never be formidable to the liberties of the people while there is a large body of citizens, little, if at all, inferior to them in discipline and the use of arms, who stand ready to defend their own rights and those of their fellow-citizens. This appears to me the only substitute that can be devised for a standing army, and the best possible security against it, if it should exist.

—Alexander Hamilton, Federalist No. 29, 1788

September 7

The foundation of our empire was not laid in the gloomy age of ignorance and superstition, but at an epoch when the rights of mankind were better understood and more clearly defined, than at any former period; the researches of the human mind, after social happiness, have been carried to a great extent, the treasures of knowledge, acquired by the labors of philosophers, sages and legislatures, through a long succession of years, are laid open for our use, and their collected wisdom may be happily

applied in the establishment of our forms of government.
. . . At this auspicious period, the United States came
into existence as a nation, and if their citizens should not
be completely free and happy, the fault will be entirely
their own.

—George Washington, Circular to the States,
June 8, 1783

September 8

The Constitution . . . meant that its coordinate branches
should be checks on each other. But the opinion which
gives to the judges the right to decide what laws are
constitutional and what not, not only for themselves in
their own sphere of action but for the legislature and
executive also in their spheres, would make the judiciary
a despotic branch.

—Thomas Jefferson to Abigail Adams,
Sept. 11, 1804

September 9

A popular government, without popular information, or
the means of acquiring it, is but a prologue to a farce
or a tragedy; or, perhaps both. Knowledge will forever
govern ignorance: And a people who mean to be their
own governors, must arm themselves with the power
which knowledge gives. A popular government without
popular information or the means of acquiring it, is but
a prologue to a farce or a tragedy or perhaps both.

—James Madison to W. T. Barry, Aug. 4, 1822

September 10

The object most interesting to me for the residue of my life, will be to see you both [his wife and daughter] developing daily those principles of virtue and goodness which will make you valuable to others and happy in yourselves, and acquiring those talents and that degree of science which will guard you at all times against ennui, the most dangerous poison of life. A mind always employed is always happy. This is the true secret, the grand recipe for felicity. . . . In a world which furnishes so many employments which are useful, and so many which are amusing, it is our own fault if we ever know what ennui is.

—Thomas Jefferson to Martha Jefferson,
May 21, 1787

September 11

The eyes of the world being thus on our country, it is put the more on its good behavior, and under the greater obligation also, to do justice to the tree of liberty by an exhibition of the fine fruits we gather from it.

—James Madison to James Monroe, Dec. 16, 1824

September 12

An entire consolidation of the states into one complete national sovereignty would imply an entire subordination of the parts; and whatever powers might remain in them, would be altogether dependent on the general will. But as the plan of the convention aims only at a partial union or consolidation, the state governments would clearly retain all the rights of sovereignty which they before had, and which were not, by that act, *exclusively* delegated to the United States.

—Alexander Hamilton, Federalist No. 32, 1788

September 13

The satisfaction arising from the indulgent opinion entertained by the American people of my conduct, will, I trust, be some security for preventing me from doing anything, which might justly incur the forfeiture of that opinion. And the consideration that human happiness and moral duty are inseparably connected, will always continue to prompt me to promote the progress of the former, by inculcating the practice of the latter.

—George Washington to the Protestant
Episcopal Church, Aug. 19, 1789

September 14

I know . . . that some honest men fear that a republican government cannot be strong, that this government is not strong enough; but would the honest patriot, in the full tide of successful experiment, abandon a government which has so far kept us free and firm on the theoretic and visionary fear that this government, the world's best hope, may by possibility want energy to preserve itself? I trust not. I believe this, on the contrary, the strongest government on earth. I believe it the only one where every man, at the call of the law, would fly to the standard of the law, and would meet invasions of the public order as his own personal concern. Sometimes it is said that man cannot be trusted with the government of himself.

Can he, then, be trusted with the government of others? Or have we found angels in the forms of kings to govern him? Let history answer this question.

—Thomas Jefferson, First Inaugural Address,
Mar. 4, 1801

September 15

It is the duty of all men in society, publicly, and at stated seasons, to worship the SUPREME BEING, the great Creator and Preserver of the universe. And no subject shall be hurt, molested, or restrained, in his person, liberty, or estate, for worshipping GOD in the manner most agreeable to the dictates of his own conscience; or for his religious profession or sentiments; provided he doth not disturb the public peace, or obstruct others in their religious worship.

—John Adams, *Thoughts on Government*, 1776

September 16

It can be of no weight to say, that the courts, on the pretense of a repugnancy, may substitute their own pleasure to the constitutional intentions of the legislature. This might as well happen in the case of two contradictory statutes; or it might as well happen in every adjudication upon any single statute. The courts must declare the sense of the law; and if they should be disposed to exercise *will* instead of *judgment*, the consequence would equally be the substitution of their pleasure to that of the legislative body.

—Alexander Hamilton, Federalist No. 78, 1788

September 17

Whilst the last members were signing it [the Constitution] Doctor Franklin looking towards the President's [George Washington's] chair, at the back of which a rising sun happened to be painted, observed to a few members near him that painters had found it difficult to distinguish in their art a rising from a setting sun. I have, said he, often and often in the course of the session, and the vicissitudes of my hopes and fears as to its issue, looked at that behind the president without being able to tell whether it was rising or setting: But now at length I have the happiness to know that it is a rising and not a setting sun.

—Recorded by James Madison, Constitutional
Convention, Sept. 17, 1787

September 18

A man's land, or merchandise, or money is called his property. . . .

A man has a property in his opinions and the free communication of them.

He has a property of peculiar value in his religious opinions, and in the profession and practice dictated by them.

He has a property very dear to him in the safety and liberty of his person.

He has an equal property in the free use of his faculties and free choice of the objects on which to employ them.

In a word, as a man is said to have a right to his property, he may be equally said to have a property in his rights.

Where an excess of power prevails, property of no sort is duly respected. No man is safe in his opinions, his person, his faculties, or his possessions. . . .

The praise of affording a just securing to property, should be sparingly bestowed on a government which, however scrupulously guarding the possessions of individuals, does not protect them in the enjoyment and communication of their opinions, in which they have an equal, and in the estimation of some, a more valuable property.

—James Madison, "Essay on Property," Mar. 1792

September 19

The spirit of encroachment tends to consolidate the powers of all the departments in one, and thus to create whatever the form of government, a real despotism. A just estimate of that love of power, and proneness to abuse it, which predominates in the human heart is sufficient to satisfy us of the truth of this position.

—George Washington, Farewell Address,
Sept. 19, 1796

September 20

Be not intimidated, therefore, by any terrors, from publishing with the utmost freedom, whatever can be warranted by the laws of your country; nor suffer yourselves to be wheedled out of your liberties by any pretenses of politeness, delicacy, or decency. These, as they are often used, are but three different names for hypocrisy, chicanery, and cowardice.

—John Adams, *A Dissertation on the
Canon and Feudal Law*, 1765

September 21

But ambitious encroachments of the federal government, on the authority of the state governments, would not excite the opposition of a single state, or of a few states only. They would be signals of general alarm. . . . But what degree of madness could ever drive the federal government to such an extremity.

—James Madison, Federalist No. 46, 1788

September 22

We have every opportunity and every encouragement before us, to form the noblest purest constitution on the face of the earth. We have it in our power to begin the world over again. A situation, similar to the present, hath not happened since the days of Noah until now. The birthday of a new world is at hand, and a race of men . . . are to receive their portion of freedom from the event of a few months.

—Thomas Paine, *Common Sense*, 1776

September 23

In Europe, charters of liberty have been granted by power. America has set the example . . . of charters of power granted by liberty. This revolution in the practice of the world, may, with an honest praise, be pronounced the most triumphant epoch of its history, and the most consoling presage of its happiness.

—James Madison, essay in *National Gazette*,
Jan. 18, 1792

September 24

Our army must undoubtedly feel fatigue, and want a re-inforcement of rest though not of valor. Our own interest and happiness call upon us to give them every support in our power, and make the burden of the day . . . as light as possible. . . .

When we look back on the dangers we have been saved from, and reflect on the success we have been blessed with, it would be sinful either to be idle or to despair. . . .

We know the cause which we are engaged in, and though a passionate fondness for it may make us grieve at every injury which threatens it, yet, when the moment of concern is over, the determination to duty returns. We are not moved by the gloomy smile of a worthless king, but by the ardent glow of generous patriotism. We fight not to enslave, but to set a country free, and to make room upon the earth for honest men to live in. In such a case we are sure that we are right; and we leave to you [British General William Howe] the despairing reflection of being the tool of a miserable tyrant.

—Thomas Paine, *American Crisis*, No. 4,
Sept. 11, 1777

September 25

There is no position which depends on clearer principles, than that every act of a delegated authority, contrary to the tenor of the commission under which it is exercised, is void. No legislative act, therefore, contrary to the Constitution, can be valid. To deny this, would be to affirm, that the deputy is greater than his principal; that the servant is above his master; that the representatives of the people are superior to the people themselves; that men acting by virtue of powers, may do not only what their powers do not authorize, but what they forbid. . . .

It is not otherwise to be supposed, that the Constitution could intend to enable the representatives of the people to substitute their *will* to that of their constituents. It is far more rational to suppose, that the courts were designed to be an intermediate body between the people and the legislature, in order, among other things, to keep the latter within the limits assigned to their authority.

—Alexander Hamilton, Federalist No. 78, 1788

September 26

Corruption in elections is the great enemy of freedom. . . . The people have almost always expected to be served gratis, and to be paid for the honor of serving them; and their applauses and adorations are bestowed too often on artifices and tricks, on hypocrisy and superstition, on flattery, bribes, and largesses. . . . When the legislature is corrupted, the people are undone.

—John Adams, *A Defence of the Constitutions of Government,* 1787

September 27

I acknowledge, in the ordinary course of government, that the exposition of the laws and Constitution devolves upon the judicial. But I beg to know upon what principle it can be contended that any one department draws from the Constitution greater powers than another in marking out the limits of the powers of the several departments.

—James Madison, speech in Congress, June 17, 1789

September 28

[When] our revolution commenced . . . we had never been permitted to exercise self-government. We established however some, although not all its important principles. The constitutions of most of our states assert, that all power is inherent in the people; that they may exercise it by themselves, in all cases to which they think themselves competent, (as in electing their functionaries executive and legislative, and deciding by a jury of themselves, in all judiciary cases in which any fact is involved,) or they may act by representatives, freely and equally chosen; that it is their right and duty to be at all times armed; that they are entitled to freedom of person, freedom of religion, freedom of property, and freedom of the press.

—Thomas Jefferson to John Cartwright,
June 5, 1824

September 29

History has informed us that bodies of men, as well as individuals, are susceptible of the spirit of tyranny. . . . Scarcely have our minds been able to emerge from the astonishment into which one stroke of parliamentary thunder has involved us, before another more heavy, and more alarming, is fallen on us. Single acts of tyranny may be ascribed to the accidental opinion of a day; but a series of oppressions, begun at a distinguished period, and pursued unalterably through every change of ministers, too plainly prove a deliberate and systematical plan of reducing us to slavery.

—Thomas Jefferson, *A Summary View of the Rights of British America*, July 1774

September 30

It may not be easy, in every possible case, to trace the line of separation between the rights of religion and the civil authority with such distinctness as to avoid collisions and doubts on unessential points. The tendency to usurpation on one side or the other, or to a corrupting coalition or alliance between them, will be best guarded against by an entire abstinence of the government from interference in any way whatsoever, beyond the necessity of preserving public order, and protecting each sect against trespasses on its legal rights by others.

—James Madison to the Reverend
Jasper Adams, Jan. 1, 1832

OCTOBER

October 1

Honor, justice, and humanity forbid us tamely to surrender that freedom which we received from our gallant ancestors, and which our innocent posterity have a right to receive from us. We cannot endure the infamy and guilt of resigning succeeding generations to that wretchedness which inevitably awaits them if we basely entail hereditary bondage on them.

> —Thomas Jefferson, "Declaration of the Causes and Necessities of Taking up Arms," July 6, 1775

October 2

However [political parties] may now and then answer popular ends, they are likely in the course of time and things, to become potent engines, by which cunning, ambitious, and unprincipled men will be enabled to subvert the power of the people and to usurp for themselves the reins of government, destroying afterwards the very engines which have lifted them to unjust dominion.

> —George Washington, Farewell Address, Sept. 19, 1796

October 3

Democracy has never been and never can be so durable as aristocracy or monarchy; but while it lasts, it is more bloody than either. . . .

Remember, democracy never lasts long. It soon wastes, exhausts, and murders itself. There never was a democracy yet that did not commit suicide. It is in vain to say that democracy is less vain, less proud, less selfish, less ambitious, or less avaricious than aristocracy or monarchy. It is not true, in fact, and nowhere appears in history. Those passions are the same in all men, under all forms of simple government, and when unchecked, produce the same effects of fraud, violence, and cruelty. When clear prospects are opened before vanity, pride, avarice, or ambition, for their easy gratification, it is hard for the most considerate philosophers and the most conscientious moralists to resist the temptation. Individuals have conquered themselves. Nations and large bodies of men, never.

—John Adams to John Taylor, Apr. 15, 1814

(Like other Founders, Adams saw great dangers in pure democracy; the U.S. Constitution instead established a democratic republic.)

October 4

I hope you are sufficiently guarded against the allurements and vanities that beset us on our first entrance on the theatre of life. . . . A watchful eye must be kept on ourselves lest while we are building ideal monuments of renown and bliss here we neglect to have our names enrolled in the annals of heaven.

—James Madison to William Bradford, Nov. 9, 1772

October 5

I dwell on this prospect [a moral people and a free government] with every satisfaction . . . : Since there is no truth more thoroughly established, than that there exists in the economy and course of nature, an indissoluble union between virtue and happiness, between duty and advantage, between the genuine maxims of an honest and magnanimous policy, and the solid rewards of public prosperity and felicity: Since we ought to be no less persuaded that the propitious smiles of Heaven, can never be expected on a nation that disregards the eternal rules of order and right, which Heaven itself has ordained: And since the preservation of the sacred fire of liberty, and the destiny of the republican model of government, are justly considered as *deeply*, perhaps as *finally* staked, on the experiment entrusted to the hands of the American people.

—George Washington, First Inaugural Address, Apr. 30, 1789

October 6

Not a place upon earth might be so happy as America. Her situation is remote from all the wrangling world, and she has nothing to do but to trade with them. A man can distinguish himself between temper and principle, and I am as confident, as I am that God governs the world, that America will never be happy till she gets clear of foreign dominion. Wars, without ceasing, will break out till that period arrives, and the continent must in the end be conqueror; for though the flame of liberty may sometimes cease to shine, the coal can never expire.

—Thomas Paine, *American Crisis*, no. 1, Dec. 1776

October 7

Our legislators are not sufficiently apprised of the rightful
limits of their power; that their true office is to declare
and enforce only our natural rights and duties, and to
take none of them from us. No man has a natural right
to commit aggression on the equal rights of another; and
this is all from which the laws ought to restrain him;
every man is under the natural duty of contributing to
the necessities of the society; and this is all the laws
should enforce on him; and, no man having a natural
right to be the judge between himself and another, it is
his natural duty to submit to the umpirage of an impartial
third. When the laws have declared and enforced all this,
they have fulfilled their functions, and the idea is quite
unfounded, that on entering into society we give up any
natural right.

—Thomas Jefferson to Francis W. Gilmer,
June 27, 1816

October 8

The blessed religion revealed in the word of God will
remain an eternal and awful monument to prove that
the best institutions may be abused by human depravity;
and that they may even, in some instances be made
subservient to the vilest of purposes. Should, hereafter,
those who are entrusted with the management of this
government, incited by the lust of power and prompted
by the supineness or venality of their constituents, over-
leap the known barriers of this Constitution and violate
the unalienable rights of humanity: it will only serve to
shew, that no compact among men (however provident
in its construction and sacred in its ratification) can be
pronounced everlasting and inviolable—and if I may so

express myself, that no wall of words—that no mound of parchment can be so formed as to stand against the sweeping torrent of boundless ambition on the one side, aided by the sapping current of corrupted morals on the other.

—George Washington, early draft of First
Inaugural Address, Apr. 1789

October 9

Let the pulpit resound with the doctrines and sentiments of religious liberty. Let us hear the danger of thralldom to our consciences, from ignorance, extreme poverty and dependence, in short from civil and political slavery. Let us see delineated before us, the true map of man. Let us hear the dignity of his nature, and the noble rank he holds among the works of God! that consenting to slavery is a sacrilegious breach of trust, as offensive in the sight of God, as it is derogatory from our own honor or interest or happiness; and that God Almighty has promulgated from heaven, liberty, peace, and good-will to man! . . . Let it be known that British liberties are not the grants of princes and parliaments.

—John Adams, *Dissertation on the
Canon and Feudal Law,* 1765

October 10

You seem to consider the federal judges as the ultimate arbiters of all constitutional questions, a very dangerous doctrine, indeed, and one which would place us under the despotism of an oligarchy. Our judges are as honest as other men, and not more so. They have with others the same passions for the party, for power and the privilege of the corps. . . . Their power is the more dangerous, as they are in office for life and not responsible, as the other functionaries are, to the elective control. The Constitution has erected no such single tribunal, knowing that to whatever hands confided, with the corruptions of time and party, its members would become despots. It has more wisely made all departments co-equal and co-sovereign within themselves.

—Thomas Jefferson to William Charles Jarvis,
Sept. 28, 1820

October 11

When the great body of the people are determined not to be imposed upon by a false glare of virtues held before their eyes, but, making up their own minds, shall impartially give in their suffrages, after their best enquiries into the characters of candidates, for those whom they judge to be the fittest persons, there will be no danger that the generous enthusiasm of freedom . . . will ever sink into the violence and rage of party, which has often proved fatal to free republics.

—Samuel Adams, in the *Boston Gazette,*
Apr. 16, 1781

October 12

I consider the foundation of the Constitution as laid on this ground that "all powers not delegated to the United States, by the Constitution, nor prohibited by it to the states, are reserved to the states or to the people" [10th Amendment]. To take a single step beyond the boundaries thus specially drawn around the powers of Congress, is to take possession of a boundless field of power, not longer susceptible of any definition.

—Thomas Jefferson, "Opinion on the Constitutionality of a National Bank," Feb. 15, 1791

October 13

The best service that can be rendered to a country, next to that of giving it liberty, is in diffusing the mental improvement equally essential to the preservation, and the enjoyment of the blessing.

—James Madison to Littleton Dennis Teackle, Mar. 29, 1826

October 14

The alternate domination of one faction over another, sharpened by the spirit of revenge, natural to party dissension, which in different ages and countries has perpetrated the most horrid enormities, is itself a frightful despotism. But this leads at length to a more formal and permanent despotism. The disorders and miseries, which result, gradually incline the minds of men to seek security and repose in the absolute power of an individual; and sooner or later the chief of some prevailing faction, more able or more fortunate than his competitors, turns this disposition to the purposes of his own elevation, on the ruins of public liberty.

—George Washington, Farewell Address, Sept. 19, 1796

October 15

If Congress can do whatever in their *discretion* can
be *done by money,* and will promote the *general welfare,*
the government is no longer a limited one possessing
enumerated powers, but an indefinite one subject to particular exceptions. It is to be remarked that the phrase
out of which this doctrine is elaborated, is copied from
the old Articles of Confederation, where it was always
understood as nothing more than a general caption to
the specified powers, and it is a fact that it was preferred
in the new instrument for that very reason as less liable
than any other to misconstruction.

—James Madison to Edmund Pendleton,
Jan. 21, 1792

October 16

No [one] on earth [is] less disposed than I am to influence the opinions of others. . . . I have been afraid to
express opinions unasked, lest I should be suspected of
wishing to direct the legislative action of members [of
Congress]. . . . I see too many proofs of the imperfection
of human reason, to entertain wonder or intolerance at
any difference of opinion on any subject; and acquiesce
in that difference as easily as on a difference of feature
or form; experience having long taught me the reason-
ableness of mutual sacrifices of opinion among those
who are to act together for any common object, and the
expediency of doing what good we can, when we cannot
do all we would wish.

—Thomas Jefferson to John Randolph,
Dec. 1, 1803

October 17

The Federalists . . . erred in relying so much on the rectitude and utility of their measures, as to have neglected the cultivation of popular favor by fair and justifiable expedients. Unluckily however for us in the competition for the passions of the people our opponents have great advantages over us; for the plain reason, that the vicious are far more active than the good passions, and that to win the latter to our side we must renounce our principles and our objects, and unite in corrupting public opinion till it becomes fit for nothing but mischief. Yet unless we can contrive to take hold of and carry along with us some strong feelings of the mind we shall in vain calculate upon any substantial or durable results.

—Alexander Hamilton to James A. Bayard,
Apr. 16, 1802

(The Federalists favored a stronger central government.
Hamilton was a founder of the Federalist Party.)

October 18

The government of the United States is a definite government, confined to specified objects. It is not like the state governments, whose powers are more general. Charity is no part of the legislative duty of the government. It would puzzle any gentleman to lay his finger on any part of the Constitution which would authorize the government to interpose in the relief of [refugees from St. Domingo, now Haiti].

—James Madison, speech in the House of
Representatives, Jan. 10, 1794

October 19

The great art of law-giving consists in balancing the poor
against the rich in the legislature, and in constituting the
legislative a perfect balance against the executive power,
at the same time that no individual or party can become
its rival. The essence of a free government consists in
an effectual control of rivalries. The executive and the
legislative powers are natural rivals; and if each has not
an effectual control over the other, the weaker will ever
be the lamb in the paws of the wolf. The nation which
will not adopt an equilibrium of power must adopt a
despotism. There is no other alternative. Rivalries must
be controlled, or they will throw all things into confusion;
and there is nothing but despotism or a balance of power
which can control them.

—John Adams, *Discourses on Davila*, 1790

October 20

The opinions of men with respect to government are
changing fast in all countries. The revolutions of America and France have thrown a beam of light over the
world, which reaches into man. The enormous expense
of governments has provoked people to think, by making
them feel; and when once the veil begins to rend, it
admits not of repair. Ignorance is of a peculiar nature;
once dispelled, it is impossible to reestablish it. It is not
originally a thing of itself, but is only the absence of
knowledge; and though man may be kept ignorant, he
cannot be made ignorant. The mind, in discovering truth,
acts in the same manner as it acts through the eye in
discovering objects; when once any object has been seen,
it is impossible to put the mind back to the same condi-

tion it was in before it saw it. . . . It has never yet been discovered how to make man unknow his knowledge, or unthink his thoughts.

—Thomas Paine, *Rights of Man,* 1791

October 21

A primary object should be the education of our youth in the science of government. In a republic, what species of knowledge can be equally important? And what duty more pressing than communicating it to those who are to be the future guardians of the liberties of the country?

—George Washington, Eighth Annual Address,
Dec. 7, 1796

October 22

A pure democracy, by which I mean a society consisting of a small number of citizens, who assemble and administer the government in person, can admit of no cure for the mischiefs of faction. . . . Democracies have ever been spectacles of turbulence and contention; have ever been found incompatible with personal security, or the rights of property; and have, in general, been as short in their lives as they have been violent in their deaths.

—James Madison, Federalist No. 10, 1787

October 23

The path of our duty is plain before us; honesty will be found on every experiment, to be the best and only true policy. Let us, then, as a nation be just; let us fulfil the public contracts which Congress [has made] with the same good faith we suppose ourselves bound to perform our private engagements.

—George Washington, Circular Letter
to the States, June 14, 1783

October 24

Dependence begets subservience and venality, suffocates the germ of virtue, and prepares fit tools for the designs of ambition. . . . It is the manners and spirit of a people which preserve a republic in vigor. A degeneracy in these is a canker which soon eats to the heart of its laws and constitution.

—Thomas Jefferson, *Notes on the
State of Virginia,* 1781

October 25

The terms "common defence and general welfare," as here used, are not novel terms, first introduced into this Constitution. They are terms familiar in their construction, and well known to the people of America. They are repeatedly found in the old Articles of Confederation, where, although they are susceptible of as great a latitude as can be given them by the context here, it was never supposed or pretended that they conveyed any such power as is now assigned to them. On the contrary, it was always considered clear and certain that the old Congress was limited to the enumerated powers, and that the enumeration limited and explained the general terms. I ask . . . whether it was ever supposed or suspected that the old Congress could give away the money of the states to bounties to encourage agriculture, or for any other purpose they pleased. If such a power had been possessed by that body, it would have been much less impotent, or have borne a very different character from that universally ascribed to it.

The novel idea now annexed to those terms, and never before entertained by the friends or enemies of the government, [would] give Congress the complete legislative power I have stated.

> —James Madison, congressional debate
> on the cod fishery bill, Feb. 7, 1792

October 26

The state governments possess inherent advantages, which will ever give them an influence and ascendancy over the national government, and will forever preclude the possibility of federal encroachments. That their liberties, indeed, can be subverted by the federal head, is repugnant to every rule of political calculation.

> —Alexander Hamilton, New York Ratifying
> Convention, June 17, 1788

October 27

The great object of my fear is the federal judiciary. That body, like gravity, ever acting, with noiseless foot, and unalarming advance, gaining ground step by step, and holding what it gains, is engulfing insidiously the special governments into the jaws of that which feeds them. . . . Let the eye of vigilance never be closed.

> —Thomas Jefferson to Judge Spencer Roane,
> Mar. 9, 1821

October 28

The sun never shined on a cause of greater worth. 'Tis not the affair of a city, a country, a province, or a kingdom, but of a continent—of at least one eighth part of the habitable globe. 'Tis not the concern of a day, a year, or an age; posterity are virtually involved in the contest, and will be more or less affected, even to the end of time, by the proceedings now. Now is the seed time of continental union, faith and honor. The least fracture now will be like a name engraved with the point of a pin on the tender rind of a young oak; The wound will enlarge with the tree, and posterity read it in full grown characters.

—Thomas Paine, *Common Sense*, 1776

October 29

As a very important source of strength and security, cherish public credit. One method of preserving it is, to use it as sparingly as possible; avoiding occasions of expense by cultivating peace, but remembering also that timely disbursements to prepare for danger frequently prevent much greater disbursements to repel it; avoiding likewise the accumulation of debt, not only by shunning occasions of expense, but by vigorous exertions in time of peace to discharge the debts, which unavoidable wars may have occasioned, not ungenerously throwing upon posterity the burthen, which we ourselves ought to bear.

—George Washington, Farewell Address,
Sept. 19, 1796

October 30

An opinion prevails that there is no longer any distinction, that the Republicans and Federalists are completely
amalgamated but it is not so. The amalgamation is of
name only, not of principle. . . . But the truth is that
finding that monarchy is a desperate wish in this country,
they rally to the point which they think next best, a
consolidated government. Their aim is now therefore to
break down the rights reserved by the constitution to
the states as a bulwark against that consolidation, the
fear of which produced the whole of the opposition to
the constitution at its birth. Hence new Republicans in
Congress, preaching the doctrines of the old Federalists.
. . . But I trust they will fail under the new, as the old
name, and that the friends of the real constitution and
union will prevail against consolidation, as they have
done against monarchism. I scarcely know myself which
is most to be deprecated, a consolidation, or dissolution
of the states. The horrors of both are beyond the reach
of human foresight.

—Thomas Jefferson to William B. Giles,
Dec. 26, 1825

October 31

Aristotle, Livy, and Harrington . . . define a republic to
be a government of laws, and not of men. . . . Metaphysi-
cians and politicians may dispute forever, but they will
never find any other moral principle or foundation of
rule or obedience, than the consent of governors and
governed.

—John Adams, *Novanglus*, Feb.–Mar. 1775

NOVEMBER

November 1

It has been observed . . . that a pure democracy, if it were practicable, would be the most perfect government. Experience has proved that no position is more false than this. The ancient democracies in which the people themselves deliberated never possessed one feature of good government. Their very character was tyranny; their figure deformity: When they assembled, the field of debate presented an ungovernable mob, not only incapable of deliberation, but prepared for every enormity.

—Alexander Hamilton, New York Ratifying
Convention, June 21, 1788

November 2

There is nothing which I dread so much as a division of the republic into two great parties, each arranged under its leader, and concerting measures in opposition to each other. This, in my humble apprehension, is to be dreaded as the greatest political evil under our Constitution.

—John Adams to Jonathan Jackson, Oct. 2, 1780

November 3

And true it is that the people, especially when moderately instructed, are the only safe, because the only honest, depositories of the public rights, and should therefore be introduced into the administration of them in every function to which they are sufficient; they will err sometimes and accidentally, but never designedly, and with a systematic and persevering purpose of overthrowing the free principles of the government.

—Thomas Jefferson to A. Coray, Oct. 31, 1823

November 4

But is there no danger when the very foundations of our civil constitution tremble? When an attempt was first made to disturb the cornerstone of the fabric, we were universally and justly alarmed. And can we be cool spectators when we see it already removed from its place? . . .

Is it a time for us to sleep when our free government is essentially changed, and a new one is forming upon a quite different system? A government without the least dependence on the people—a government under the absolute control of a minister of state. . . .

Have we not already seen specimens of what we are to expect under such a government? . . .

But let us be upon our guard against even a negative submission, for . . . if we are voluntarily silent as the conspirators would have us to be, it will be considered as an approbation of the change.

—Samuel Adams, in *Boston Gazette,* Oct. 14, 1771

November 5

These are the times that try men's souls. The summer soldier and the sunshine patriot will, in this crisis, shrink from the service of their country; but he that stands by it now, deserves the love and thanks of man and woman. Tyranny, like hell, is not easily conquered; yet we have this consolation with us, that the harder the conflict, the more glorious the triumph. What we obtain too cheap, we esteem too lightly: it is dearness only that gives everything its value. Heaven knows how to put a proper price upon its goods; and it would be strange indeed if so celestial an article as *freedom* should not be highly rated.

—Thomas Paine, *American Crisis,* no. 1,
Dec. 23, 1776

November 6

There is danger from all men. The only maxim of a free government ought to be to trust no man living with power to endanger the public liberty. . . . All the great kingdoms of Europe have once been free. But that they have lost their liberties, by the ignorance, the weakness, the inconstancy, and disunion of the people. Let us guard against these dangers, let us be firm and stable, as wise as serpents and as harmless as doves, but as daring and intrepid as heroes. . . . When the popular power becomes grasping, and eager after augmentation, or for amplification, beyond its proper weight, or line, it becomes as dangerous as any other.

—John Adams, notes for an oration at Braintree,
Spring 1772

November 7

It is the duty of every man to render to the Creator such homage, and such only, as he believes to be acceptable to him. This duty is precedent both in order of time and degree of obligation, to the claims of civil society. Before any man can be considered as a member of civil society, he must be considered as a subject of the Governor of the Universe: And if a member of civil society, who enters into any subordinate association, must always do it with a reservation of his duty to the general authority; much more must every man who becomes a member of any particular civil society, do it with a saving of his allegiance to the Universal Sovereign. We maintain therefore that in matters of religion, no man's right is abridged by the institution of civil society, and that religion is wholly exempt from its cognizance.

—James Madison, "Memorial and Remonstrance against Religious Assessments," June 20, 1785

November 8

We have heard of the impious doctrine in the old world, that the people were made for kings, not kings for the people. Is the same doctrine to be revived in the new, in another shape—that the solid happiness of the people is to be sacrificed to the views of political institutions of a different form? It is too early for politicians to presume on our forgetting that the public good, the real welfare of the great body of the people, is the supreme object to be pursued; and that no form of government whatever has any other value than as it may be fitted for the attainment of this object.

—James Madison, Federalist No. 45, 1788

November 9

Democracy will soon degenerate into an anarchy, such an anarchy that every man will do what is right in his own eyes and no man's life or property or reputation or liberty will be secure, and every one of these will soon mold itself into a system of subordination of all the moral virtues and intellectual abilities, all the powers of wealth, beauty, wit and science, to the wanton pleasures, the capricious will, and the execrable cruelty of one or a very few.

—John Adams, "An Essay on Man's
Lust for Power," Aug. 29, 1763

November 10

It requires but a very small glance of thought to perceive, that although laws made in one generation often continue in force through succeeding generations, yet that they continue to derive their force from the consent of the living. A law not repealed continues in force, not because it cannot be repealed, but because it is not repealed; and the non-repealing passes for consent.

—Thomas Paine, *Rights of Man,* 1791

November 11

We took the liberty to make some enquiries concerning the ground of their pretensions to make war upon nations who had done them no injury, and observed that we considered all mankind as our friends who had done us no wrong, nor had given us any provocation.

The ambassador [of Tripoli] answered us that it was

founded on the laws of their prophet, that it was written in their Koran, that all nations who should not have acknowledged their authority were sinners, that it was their right and duty to make war upon them wherever they could be found, and to make slaves of all they could take as prisoners, and that every Musselman [Muslim] who should be slain in battle was sure to go to paradise.

—John Adams and Thomas Jefferson to John Jay,
Mar. 28, 1786

(Adams and Jefferson were sent by Congress to deal with
representatives of the North African Barbary States, which
were supporting pirates that were attacking American
ships and ransoming or enslaving the crews.)

November 12

I am . . . concerned to see . . . a germ of division which, if not smothered, will continue. . . . If we do not learn to sacrifice small differences of opinion, we can never act together. Every man cannot have his way in all things. If his own opinion prevails at some times, he should acquiesce on seeing that of others preponderate at others. Without this mutual disposition we are disjointed individuals, but not a society. . . . I am proceeding [as president] with deliberation and inquiry to do what I think just to both [parties] and conciliatory to both. The greatest good we can do our country is to heal its party divisions and make them one people. I do not speak of their leaders who are incurable, but of the honest and well-intentioned body of the people. . . . Both sects are . . . entitled to the confidence of their fellow citizens. Not so their quondam leaders. . . . They have a right to tolerance, but neither to confidence nor power.

—Thomas Jefferson to John Dickinson, July 23, 1801

November 13

Were the talents and virtues which heaven has bestowed on men given merely to make them more obedient drudges, to be sacrificed to the follies and ambition of a few? Or, were not the noble gifts so equally dispensed with a divine purpose and law, that they should as nearly as possible be equally exerted, and the blessings of Providence be equally enjoyed by all?

—Samuel Adams, speech, Pennsylvania State House, Philadelphia, Aug. 1, 1776

November 14

Our obligations to our country never cease but with our lives. We ought to do all we can. . . . The miserable struggle for place and power must be laid aside, and heart and hand united for defense. . . . [We] can do much to guard against that avarice which is our national sin, which is most likely to draw down Judgment.

—John Adams to Benjamin Rush, Apr. 18, 1808

November 15

When the representative body have lost the confidence of their constituents, when they have notoriously made sale of their most valuable rights, when they have assumed to themselves powers which the people never put into their hands, then indeed their continuing in office becomes dangerous to the state, and calls for an exercise of the power of dissolution.

—Thomas Jefferson, *A Summary View of the Rights of British America*, July 1774

November 16

Man did not enter into society to become worse than he was before, nor to have fewer rights than he had before, but to have those rights better secured. His natural rights are the foundation of all his civil rights. . . . Natural rights are those which appertain to man in right of his existence. Of this kind are all the intellectual rights, or rights of the mind, and also all those rights of acting as an individual for his own comfort and happiness, which are not injurious to the natural rights of others. Civil rights are those which appertain to man in right of his being a member of society. Every civil right has for its foundation some natural right pre-existing in the individual, but to the enjoyment of which his individual power is not, in all cases, sufficiently competent. Of this kind are all those which relate to security and protection.

—Thomas Paine, *Rights of Man,* 1791

November 17

The common and continual mischiefs of the spirit of party are sufficient to make it the interest and the duty of a wise people to discourage and restrain it. It serves always to distract the public councils and enfeeble the public administration. It agitates the community with ill-founded jealousies and false alarms, kindles the animosity of one part against another, foments occasionally riot and insurrection. It opens the door to foreign influence and corruption, which find a facilitated access to the government itself through the channels of party passion.

—George Washington, Farewell Address,
Sept. 19, 1796

November 18

I entirely concur in the propriety of resorting to the sense in which the Constitution was accepted and ratified by the nation. In that sense alone it is the legitimate Constitution. And if that be not the guide in expounding it, there can be no security for a consistent and stable [government], more than for a faithful exercise of its powers. If the meaning of the text be sought in the changeable meaning of the words composing it, it is evident that the shape and attributes of the government must partake of the changes to which the words and phrases of all living languages are constantly subject. What a metamorphosis would be produced in the code of law if all its ancient phraseology were to be taken in its modern sense!

—James Madison to Henry Lee, June 25, 1824

November 19

Nothing can appear more contradictory than the principles on which the old governments began, and the condition to which society, civilization and commerce are capable of carrying mankind. Government, on the old system, is an assumption of power, for the aggrandizement of itself; on the new, a delegation of power for the common benefit of society. The former supports itself by keeping up a system of war; the later promotes a system of peace, as the true means of enriching a nation. The one encourages national prejudices; the other promotes universal society, as the means of universal commerce. The one measures its prosperity, by the quantity of revenue it extorts; the other proves its excellence, by the small quantity of taxes it requires.

—Thomas Paine, *Rights of Man*, 1791

November 20

I join cordially in admiring and revering the Constitution
of the United States, the result of the collected wisdom
of our country. That wisdom has committed to us the
important task of proving by example that a government,
if organized in all its parts on the representative principle
unadulterated by the infusion of spurious elements, if
founded, not in the fears and follies of man, but on his
reason, on his sense of right, on the predominance of the
social over his dissocial passions, may be so free as to
restrain him in no moral right, and so firm as to protect
him from every moral wrong.

—Thomas Jefferson to Amos Marsh, Nov. 20, 1801

November 21

Let us with caution indulge the supposition, that morality can be maintained without religion. Whatever may
be conceded to the influence of refined education on
minds of peculiar structure, reason and experience both
forbid us to expect, that national morality can prevail in
exclusion of religious principle.

—George Washington, Farewell Address,
Sept. 19, 1796

November 22

I sincerely wish you may find it convenient to come
here [Paris, France]. The pleasure of the trip will be less
than you expect but the utility greater. It will make you
adore your own country, its soil, its climate, its equality,
liberty, laws, people, and manners. . . . How little do my

countrymen know what precious blessings they are in possession of, and which no other people on earth enjoy! While we shall see multiplied instances of Europeans going to live in America, I will venture to say no man now living will ever see an instance of an American removing to settle in Europe and continuing there. Come then and see the proofs of this, and on your return add your testimony to that of every thinking American, in order to satisfy our countrymen how much it is their interest to preserve uninfected by contagion those peculiarities in their government and manners to which they are indebted for these blessings.

—Thomas Jefferson to James Monroe, June 17, 1785

November 23

The consequences arising from the continual accumulation of public debts in other countries ought to admonish us to be careful to prevent their growth in our own. The national defense must be provided for as well as the support of government; but both should be accomplished as much as possible by immediate taxes, and as little as possible by loans.

—John Adams, First Address to Congress,
Nov. 23, 1797

November 24

The capital and leading object of the constitution was to leave with the states all authorities which respected their own citizens only, and to transfer to the United States those which respected citizens of foreign or other states: to make us several as to ourselves, but one as to

all others. In the latter case, then, constructions should
lean to the general jurisdiction, if the words will bear
it; and in favor of the states in the former, if possible
to be so construed.

—Thomas Jefferson to William Johnson,
June 12, 1823

November 25

A single assembly will never be a steady guardian of
the laws, if Machiavel is right, when he says, Men are
never good but through necessity: on the contrary, when
good and evil are left to their choice, they will not fail to
throw everything into disorder and confusion. Hunger
and poverty may make men industrious, but laws only
can make them good; for, if men were so of themselves,
there would be no occasion for laws; but, as the case is
far otherwise, they are absolutely necessary.

—John Adams, *A Defence of the Constitutions
of Government*, 1787

November 26

Whereas it is the duty of all nations to acknowledge
the providence of Almighty God, to obey His will, to
be grateful for his benefits, and humbly to implore His
protection and favor. . . . Now, therefore, I do recommend
and assign Thursday, the twenty-sixth day of November
next, to be devoted by the people of these United States
. . . that we then may all unite unto him our sincere
and humble thanks for His kind care and protection of
the people of this country previous to their becoming
a nation; for the signal and manifold mercies and the

favorable interpositions of His providence in the course and conclusion of the late war; for the great degree of tranquility, union, and plenty which we have since enjoyed; for the peaceable and rational manner in which we have been enabled to establish constitutions of government for our safety and happiness, and . . . for the civil and religious liberty with which we are blessed.

—George Washington, Thanksgiving Proclamation,
Oct. 3, 1789

November 27

If Congress can employ money indefinitely to the general welfare, and are the sole and supreme judges of the general welfare, they may take the care of religion into their own hands; they may appoint teachers in every state, county, and parish, and pay them out of their public treasury; they may take into their own hands the education of children, establishing in like manner schools throughout the union; they may assume the provision for the poor; they may undertake the regulation of all roads other than post-roads; in short, everything, from the highest object of state legislation down to the most minute object of police, would be thrown under the power of Congress; for every object I have mentioned would admit of the application of money, and might be called, if Congress pleased, provisions for the general welfare. . . .

Were the power of Congress to be established in the latitude contended for, it would subvert the very foundations, and transmute the very nature of the limited government established by the people of America.

—James Madison, congressional debate
on the cod fishery bill, Feb. 7, 1792

November 28

The origin of all civil government, justly established,
must be a voluntary compact, between the rulers and
the ruled; and must be liable to such limitations, as are
necessary for the security of the *absolute rights* of the
latter; for what original title can any man or set of men
have, to govern others, except their own consent? To
usurp dominion over a people, in their own despite, or to
grasp at a more extensive power than they are willing to
entrust, is to violate that law of nature, which gives every
man a right to his personal liberty; and can, therefore,
confer no obligation to obedience.

—Alexander Hamilton, "The Farmer Refuted,"
Feb. 23, 1775

November 29

A revolution in the state of civilization is the necessary
companion of revolutions in the system of government. If
a revolution in any country be from bad to good, or from
good to bad, the state of what is called civilization in that
country, must be made conformable thereto, to give that
revolution effect. Despotic government supports itself by
abject civilization, in which debasement of the human
mind, and wretchedness in the mass of the people, are
the chief criterions. Such governments consider man
merely as an animal; that the exercise of intellectual
faculty is not his privilege; *that he has nothing to do with
the laws but to obey them;* and they politically depend
more upon breaking the spirit of the people by poverty,
than they fear enraging it by desperation.

—Thomas Paine, *Agrarian Justice*, 1797

November 30

What ignorant puppets we are! how we grope in the dark! and what empty phantoms we chase! You are not singular in your suspicions that you know but little. The longer I live, the more I read, the more patiently I think, and the more anxiously I inquire, the less I seem to know. . . . Do justly. Love mercy. Walk humbly. This is enough.

—John Adams to Caroline Amelia Smith
De Windt, Jan. 24, 1820

DECEMBER

December 1

As no truth is more clearly taught in the Volume of Inspiration, . . . than that a deep sense and a due acknowledgement of the growing providence of a Supreme Being and of the accountableness of men to Him as the searcher of hearts and righteous distributer of rewards and punishments are conducive equally to the happiness of individuals and to the well-being of communities, . . . I have thought proper to recommend, . . . a day of solemn humiliation, fasting and prayer; that the citizens on that day . . . call to mind our numerous offenses against the most high God, . . . implore his pardoning mercy, through the Great Mediator and Redeemer, for our past transgressions, and that through the grace of His Holy Spirit, we may be disposed and enabled to yield a more suitable obedience to his righteous requisitions in time to come; that He would interpose to arrest the progress of that impiety and licentiousness in principle and practice so offensive to Himself and so ruinous to mankind; that He would make us deeply sensible that "righteousness exalteth a nation but sin is a reproach to any people" (Proverbs 14:34).

—John Adams, Proclamation for
National Fast Day, Mar. 6, 1799

December 2

The great desideratum in government is, so to modify the sovereignty as that it may be sufficiently neutral between different parts of the society to control one part from invading the rights of another, and at the same time sufficiently controlled itself, from setting up an interest adverse to that of the entire Society.

—James Madison to Thomas Jefferson,
Oct. 24, 1787

December 3

In no part of the constitution is more wisdom to be found than in the clause which confides the question of war or peace to the legislature, and not to the executive department. Beside the objection to such a mixture of heterogeneous powers: the trust and the temptation would be too great for any one man. . . . War is in fact the true nurse of executive aggrandizement. In war a physical force is to be created, and it is the executive will which is to direct it. In war the public treasures are to be unlocked, and it is the executive hand which is to dispense them. In war the honors and emoluments of office are to be multiplied; and it is the executive patronage under which they are to be enjoyed. It is in war, finally, that laurels are to be gathered, and it is the executive brow they are to encircle. The strongest passions, and most dangerous weaknesses of the human breast; ambition, avarice, vanity, the honorable or venial love of fame, are all in conspiracy against the desire and duty of peace.

—Alexander Hamilton, *The Pacificus-Helvidius Debates*, 1793–1794

December 4

If Congress were a permanent body, there would be more reason in being jealous of giving it powers. But its members are chosen annually [under the Articles of Confederation]. . . . They are of the people, and return again to mix with the people, having no more durable preeminence than the different grains of sand in an hourglass. Such an assembly cannot easily become dangerous to liberty. They are the servants of the people, sent together to do the people's business, and promote the public welfare; their powers must be sufficient, or their duties cannot be performed. They have no profitable appointments, but a mere payment of daily wages, such as are scarcely equivalent to their expenses; so that, having no chance for great places, and enormous salaries or pensions, as in some countries, there is no triguing or bribing for elections.

—Benjamin Franklin to George Whatley,
May 23, 1785

December 5

It has ever been my hobby-horse to see rising in America an empire of liberty, and a prospect of two or three hundred millions of freemen, without one noble or one king among them. You say it is impossible. If I should agree with you in this, I would still say, let us try the experiment, and preserve our equality as long as we can.

A better system of education for the common people might preserve them long from such artificial inequalities as are prejudicial to society, by confounding the natural distinctions of right and wrong, virtue and vice.

—John Adams to Count Sarsfield, Feb. 3, 1786

December 6

The true foundation of republican government is the equal right of every citizen, in his person and property, and in their management. Try by this, as a tally, every provision of our constitution, and see if it hangs directly on the will of the people. . . . [The] object is to secure self-government by the republicanism of our constitution, as well as by the spirit of the people; and to nourish and perpetuate that spirit.

—Thomas Jefferson to H. Tompkinson
(aka Samuel Kercheval), July 12, 1816

December 7

The state governments may be regarded as constituent and essential parts of the federal government; whilst the latter is nowise essential to the operation or organization of the former. . . .The operations of the federal government will be most extensive and important in times of war and danger; those of the state governments, in times of peace and security.

—James Madison, Federalist No. 45, 1788

December 8

But killing one tyrant only makes way for worse, unless the people have sense, spirit and honesty enough to establish and support a constitution guarded at all points against the tyranny of the one, the few, and the many. Let it be the study, therefore, of lawgivers and philosophers, to enlighten the people's understandings and improve their morals, by good and general education; to enable them to comprehend the scheme of government, and to know upon what points their liberties depend; to dissipate those vulgar prejudices and popular superstitions that oppose themselves to good government; and to teach them that obedience to the laws is as indispensable in them as in lords and kings.

—John Adams, *A Defence of the Constitutions of Government*, 1787

December 9

It is the duty of mankind on all suitable occasions to acknowledge their dependence on the Divine Being . . . [that] Almighty God would mercifully interpose and still the rage of war among the nations . . . [and that] He would take this province under his protection, confound the designs and defeat the attempts of its enemies, and unite our hearts and strengthen our hands in every undertaking that may be for the public good, and for our defense and security in this time of danger.

—Benjamin Franklin, proclamation of Pennsylvania's first Fast Day, 1748

December 10

After twenty years' confirmation of the federal system by the voice of the nation, declared through the medium of elections, we find the judiciary on every occasion, still driving us into consolidation. . . . The Constitution . . . is a mere thing of wax in the hands of the judiciary which they may twist and shape into any form they please.

—Thomas Jefferson to Judge Spencer Roane, Sept. 6, 1819

December 11

This assembly doth explicitly and peremptorily declare, that it views the powers of the federal government, as resulting from the compact, to which the states are parties, as limited by the plain sense and intention of the instrument constituting the compact; as no further valid than they are authorized by the grants enumerated in that compact; and that in case of deliberate, palpable, and dangerous exercise of other powers, not granted by the said compact, the states who are parties thereto, have the right, and are in duty bound, to interpose, for arresting the progress of the evil, and for maintaining within their respective limits, the authorities, rights and liberties appertaining to them.

—James Madison, "Virginia Resolution of 1798,"
Dec. 1798

December 12

It seems to have been reserved to the people of this country, by their conduct and example, to decide the important question, whether societies of men are really capable or not of establishing good government from reflection and choice, or whether they are forever destined to depend for their political constitutions on accident and force. If there be any truth in the remark, the crisis at which we are arrived may with propriety be regarded as the era in which that decision is to be made; and a wrong election of the part we shall act may, in this view, deserve to be considered as the general misfortune of mankind.

—Alexander Hamilton, Federalist No. 1, 1787

December 13

When the spirit of liberty, which now animates our hearts and gives success to our arms, is extinct, . . . contemplate the mangled bodies of your countrymen, and then say, What should be the reward of such sacrifices? Bid us and our posterity bow the knee, supplicate the friendship, and plough, and sow, and reap, to glut the avarice of the men who have let loose on us the dogs of war to riot in our blood and hunt us from the face of the earth? If ye love wealth better than liberty, the tranquility of servitude than the animating contest of freedom—go from us in peace. We ask not your counsels or arms. Crouch down and lick the hands that feed you. May your chains sit lightly upon you, and may posterity forget that ye were our countrymen!

—Samuel Adams, speech, Pennsylvania State House, Philadelphia, Aug. 1, 1776

December 14

What is to be the consequence, in case the Congress shall misconstrue this part [the necessary and proper clause] of the Constitution and exercise powers not warranted by its true meaning, I answer the same as if they should misconstrue or enlarge any other power vested in them . . . the success of the usurpation will depend on the executive and judiciary departments, which are to expound and give effect to the legislative acts; and in a last resort a remedy must be obtained from the people, who can by the elections of more faithful representatives, annul the acts of the usurpers.

—James Madison, Federalist No. 44, 1788

December 15

Time indeed changes manners and notions, and so far we must expect institutions to bend to them. But time produces also corruption of principles, and against this it is the duty of good citizens to be ever on the watch, and if the gangrene is to prevail at last, let the day be kept off as long as possible. We see already germs of this, as might be expected. But we are not the less bound to press against them. The multiplication of public offices, increase of expense beyond income, growth and entailment of a public debt, are indications soliciting the employment of the pruning-knife.

—Thomas Jefferson to Judge Spencer Roane,
Mar. 9, 1821

December 16

Moderation in every nation is a virtue. In weak or young nations, it is often wise to take every chance by patience and address to divert hostility and in this view to *hold parley* with insult and injury—but to *capitulate* with oppression, rather to surrender at discretion to it is in any nation that has any power of resistance as foolish as it contemptible. The honor of a nation is its life. Deliberately to abandon it is to commit an act of political suicide. There is treason in the sentiment avowed in the language of some, and betrayal by the conduct of others, that we ought to bear anything from [another nation] rather than go to war with her. The nation which can prefer disgrace to danger is prepared for a *master* and deserves one.

—Alexander Hamilton to the *New York Daily Advertiser*, Feb. 21, 1797

December 17

Equal laws protecting equal rights, are found as they ought to be presumed, the best guarantee of loyalty, and love of country; as well as best calculated to cherish that mutual respect and good will among citizens of every religious denomination which are necessary to social harmony and most favorable to the advancement of truth.

—James Madison to Jacob de la Motta, Aug. 7, 1820

December 18

My construction of the constitution is very different from that you quote. It is that each department is truly independent of the others, and has an equal right to decide for itself what is the meaning of the constitution in the cases submitted to its action; and especially, where it is to act ultimately and without appeal.

—Thomas Jefferson to Samuel Adams Wells,
May 12, 1819

December 19

For if experience has ever taught a truth, it is that a plurality in the supreme executive will forever split into discordant factions, distract the nation, annihilate its energies, and force the nation to rally under a single head, generally an usurper. We have, I think, fallen on the happiest of all modes of constituting the executive, that of easing and aiding our president, by permitting him to choose secretaries of state, of finance, of war, and of the navy, with whom he may advise, either separately or all together, and remedy their divisions by adopting or controlling their opinions at his discretion; this saves the nation from the evils of a divided will, and secures to it a steady march in the systematic course which the president may have adopted for that of his administration.

—Thomas Jefferson to A. Coray, Oct. 31, 1823

December 20

The House of Representatives . . . can make no law which will not have its full operation on themselves and their friends, as well as the great mass of society. This has always been deemed one of the strongest bonds by which human policy can connect the rulers and the people together. It creates between them that communion of interest, and sympathy of sentiments, of which few governments have furnished examples; but without which every government degenerates into tyranny.

—James Madison, Federalist No. 57, 1788

December 21

I agree to this Constitution, with all its faults—if they are such; because I think a general government necessary for us, and there is no form of government but what may be a blessing to the people, if well administered; and I believe, farther, that this is likely to be well administered for a course of years, and can only end in despotism, as other forms have done before it, when the people shall become so corrupted as to need despotic government, being incapable of any other.

—Benjamin Franklin, Constitutional Convention,
Sept. 17, 1787

December 22

I ever feel myself hurt when I hear the union, that great palladium of our liberty and safety, the least irreverently spoken of. It is the most sacred thing in the constitution of America, and that which every man should be most proud and tender of. Our citizenship in the United States is our national character. Our citizenship in any particular state is only our local distinction. By the latter we are known at home, by the former to the world. Our great title is AMERICANS—our inferior one varies with the place.

—Thomas Paine, *American Crisis*, no. 13,
Apr. 19, 1783

December 23

In framing a government which is to be administered by men over men, the great difficulty lies in this: you must first enable the government to control the governed; and in the next place oblige it to control itself. A dependence on the people is, no doubt, the primary control on the government; but experience has taught mankind the necessity of auxiliary precautions.

—James Madison, Federalist No. 51, 1788

December 24

Notwithstanding the general progress made within the two last centuries in favor of this branch of liberty, and the full establishment of it, in some parts of our country, there remains in others a strong bias towards the old error, that without some sort of alliance or coalition between government and religion neither can be duly supported. . . . I have no doubt that every new example, will succeed, as every past one has done, in shewing that religion and government will both exist in greater purity, the less they are mixed together. . . . We are teaching the world the great truth that governments do better without kings and nobles than with them. The merit will be doubled by the other lesson that religion flourishes in greater purity, without than with the aid of government.

—James Madison to Edward Livingston,
July 10, 1822

December 25

How many observe Christ's birthday! How few, his precepts! O! 'tis easier to keep holidays than commandments.

—Benjamin Franklin, *Poor Richard's Almanack*, 1743

December 26

Power is intoxicating; and men legally vested with it, too often discover a disposition to make an ill use of it. . . . I hope our countrymen will always keep a watchful eye over the public conduct of those whom they exalt to power, making at the same time every just allowance for the imperfections of human nature; and I pray God we may never see men filling the sacred seats of government, who are either wanting in adequate abilities, or influenced by any views, motives, or feelings separate from the public welfare.

—Samuel Adams to James Warren, Oct. 24, 1780

December 27

Liberty can have nothing to fear from the judiciary alone, but would have everything to fear from its union with either of the other departments. . . . The complete independence of the courts of justice is peculiarly essential in a limited constitution. By a limited constitution, I understand one which contains certain specified exceptions to the legislative authority. . . . Limitations of this kind can be preserved in practice no other way than through the medium of the courts of justice; whose duty it must be to declare all acts contrary to the manifest tenor of the Constitution void. Without this, all the reservations of particular rights or privileges would amount to nothing.

—Alexander Hamilton, Federalist No. 78, 1788

December 28

I turn with the warm ardor of a friend to those who have nobly stood, and are yet determined to stand the matter out [i.e., the Revolutionary War]: I call not upon a few, but upon all: not on *this* state or *that* state, but on *every* state: up and help us; lay your shoulders to the wheel; better have too much force than too little, when so great an object is at stake. Let it be told to the future world, that in the depth of winter, when nothing but hope and virtue could survive, that the city and the country, alarmed at one common danger, came forth to meet and to repulse it. . . . Throw not the burden of the day upon Providence, but *"show your faith by your works,"* that God may bless you.

—Thomas Paine, *American Crisis,* no. 1,
Dec. 23, 1776

December 29

The great leading objects of the federal government, in which revenue is concerned, are to maintain domestic peace, and provide for the common defense. In these are comprehended the regulation of commerce that is, the whole system of foreign intercourse; the support of armies and navies, and of the civil administration.

—Alexander Hamilton, Remarks in the New York
Ratifying Convention, June 27, 1788

December 30

Its [the Constitution's] principle is that of a separation of legislative, executive, and judiciary functions, except in cases specified. If this principle be not expressed in direct terms, it is clearly the spirit of the Constitution, and it ought to be so commented and acted on by every friend of free government.

—Thomas Jefferson to James Madison,
Jan. 22, 1797

December 31

My granddaughters . . . are amusing themselves with blowing bubbles with soap suds, with a tobacco pipe, a diversion that I practiced myself with great delight, about seventy years ago, but which I never thought it worthwhile to teach to my children or grandchildren. Yet I know not whether it would not have been a good allegorical lesson. They fill the air of the room with their bubbles, their air balloons, which roll and shine reflecting the light of the fire and candles, and are very beautiful.

There can be no more perfect emblem of the physical and political and theological scenes of human life.

Morality only is eternal. All the rest is balloon and bubble from the cradle to the grave.

—John Adams to John Quincy Adams, Mar. 13, 1813